THE NOVELS AND PLAYS
OF CHARLES MORGAN

CHARLES MORGAN

THE NOVELS AND PLAYS

OF

CHARLES MORGAN

by

HENRY CHARLES DUFFIN

BOWES & BOWES

LONDON

CONTENTS

ACKNOWLEDGMENTS

I wish to express my thanks to Mr Christopher Medley, Charles Morgan's literary executor, for permission to quote from the novels and plays; this permission was readily acceded to by Mrs Morgan and by Messrs Macmillan, the publishers of Charles Morgan's works. I am also grateful to Mrs Morgan, not only for much kind interest and encouragement, but for supplying a photograph of Charles Morgan, taken by M. Roland d'Ursel of Brussels, and allowing me to use it as a frontispiece.

To my wife

PREFACE

It is Hermann Keyserling, that subtle and forgotten philosopher, who says that great spirits should not concern themselves with refutation. Not being a great spirit, I am exempt from this prohibition, which in any case applies to refutation of charges against the great spirit itself, but I must admit that, though the conception of this book originated years ago in my vast admiration for Morgan's work, the desire to write it has been sharpened by the studied neglect, in more recent years, of the critics. It is astonishing that anyone could compile a history of the English novel in the Twentieth Century without mentioning Charles Morgan, yet Mr Walter Allen and others have contrived to do this, and the obituary notices were full of incredibly obtuse depreciation. Reviews of individual novels have, from the beginning, been generous and penetrating,* and Morgan's audience has been not only fit but something more than few, but one gentleman, not long ago, put it on record that his idea of hell would include 'listening to a reading of the novels of Charles Morgan'. However, as this gentleman was a subscriber to the *New Statesman*, and named as another infernal ingredient that he should have to suffer the continued presence of his wife, we may take it that his literary taste is as high as his manners are exquisite.

To me it seems incontrovertible that, as Hardy handed on the torch of the great novel to Conrad, so Conrad handed it on to Morgan.† I am not claiming equality for Morgan with either of these his predecessors: we are too close to him to be sure about

* Thus: 'A great novel and a beautiful one', 'Strangely profound, wise, courageous and beautiful', 'Mr Morgan writes about Truth as other men write about murder', 'Probably the most distinguished living master of English prose'. Moreover, continental critics have never faltered in their high and discriminating appreciation.

† Miss Clemence Dane, in a radio talk, boldly gave it as her opinion that Morgan is the greatest novelist since Hardy.

that, one way or the other. Perhaps, at their occasional best, Barrie, Bennett, Wells, Kipling, Galsworthy may approach or attain Morgan's level, but Morgan alone has produced a complete line of masterpieces, in the novel and the drama, artistically admirable, of profound significance, and of great and varied narrative power.

The line begins with *Portrait in a Mirror*, published in 1929, but Morgan had already written two novels which he did not choose to reprint, and which I have not considered in the following pages. They were *The Gunroom* and *My Name is Legion. The Gunroom*, published in 1919, is a documentary of service in the Navy, from the midshipman's point of view, in the years just before 1918, with a straightforward love-story not unskilfully woven in. (Before and during the First World War Morgan was himself in the Navy.) It depicts the sadistic maltreatment of junior midshipmen by their seniors, does not neglect to record the admirable relations that could exist with the higher officers when these were humane men, and shows that even under the best of conditions then obtaining, the deadening confinement and spiritual limitations were intolerable for a sensitive young man with the slightest leanings to culture. The Admiralty frowned upon the book's revelations, and — together with the exigencies of two wars and the general growth of humanitarianism — *The Gunroom* must have contributed to the much improved conditions that now prevail (a similar change has happened in boarding-schools, of course). But, apart from a vivid phrase or two and an occasional flight of inspired thought, there is no sign of the writer of the *Portrait*. This is again entirely true of *My Name is Legion*, written between 1919 and 1924. Its chief character, Irma Pennell, seems to possess some sort of supernatural power, and is both unattractive and unconvincing. The book begins in a simple strain, with rustics obviously imitated from Hardy, but gathers complexity as it goes along, and there are a few passages of admirable dialogue and, towards the end, some painful scenes done with moderate power. The conclusion is full of an unexpected beauty and peace, the circumstances of unbearable tension under which the greater part of the story was written having been released by a combination of happy changes in the writer's life. But *My Name is Legion* is the kind of novel of which many hundreds are published every year, and is much less competently written than most of them. The marvel is that the uncritical amateur who wrote the novel should have achieved in the next five years (years of security, happiness, and freedom from spiritual strain, with the severe discipline afforded by responsible work as a dramatic critic) the accomplished style and mastery of character and construction that make *Portrait in a Mirror* the work of genius that it undeniably is.

The term 'genius' is one that should not be lightly thrown about, but I believe the expression 'a work of genius' can be applied to all Morgan's novels, after the two 'prentice works and excepting *The Empty Room*, and to all the plays. I should like to explain why I am so sure of this. Matthew Arnold advised anyone who wished to judge the quality of a new poem to have in mind certain lines from the supreme classics, which were to be used as 'touch-stones'. My approach to any written work is similar (after the preliminary test of enjoyment, which may let through books of every grade, from *The Prisoner of Zenda* to *The Dynasts*). I ask whether it has the 'feel' of a classic; whether it arouses (in the case of a novel) the same kind of satisfaction as *Esmond, Middlemarch, The Mayor of Casterbridge*; whether it seems likely, as these have done, to endure the waves and winds of time. Apart from this, I am not in favour of the comparative estimate, and in the following pages I have not asked whether the novels I am considering are the equals of, or in any way resemble, the works of the Russians, the French, or any contemporary English or American novelist.

It will probably be admitted that this standard of judgment is a reasonable one, even if the result of my application of it may not be accepted. But I have other more personal criteria. I (who am no longer young and was never very angry) like a book that makes me feel 'good', not degraded. The *Times* obituary notice said: 'Readers of Mr Graham Greene, Mr Angus Wilson and the like had little patience with a view of life so obstinately elevated.' Now I prefer an elevated view of life, just as I prefer living in the Lake District to living in the Potteries, and would rather swim in the sea than in a slimy pond. I read Mr Graham Greene's novels with admiration, but I feel I must take a bath afterwards. I do not believe an elevated view of life means a sacrifice of truth. I have found more beauty than sordidness in life, and I believe beauty to be the more important, the more permanent, element. I accept Plato's conception of literature as the creative revelation of the ideal activity at work in human life. Morgan was a Platonist, and if his world seems to be idealized that is because he believed, as I do, that the ideal is the real.

Much of what we find in Morgan, whether we like or dislike it, is explained when we say, as he said of himself, that he was a romantic. Books have been written about romanticism and classicism, but it will suffice to note that the term romanticism connotes imagination — as opposed to reason — and freedom — as opposed to authority. Morgan has described himself, in the essay prefixed to *The Flashing Stream*, as 'one who thinks of himself first and last as an imaginative writer'; and he elsewhere asserts that romantics, 'wishing to discover an obedience which is freedom ... look for authority within themselves'. The best of the essays in the volume called *Liberties of the Mind* are those in which Morgan (imaginatively) argues the case for romanticism. Intrinsic romanticism, he suggests, is a condition of the whole man. Romanticism is not itself a religion but, like life, one of the ways in which religion may be expressed, an instrument of the spirit. Penetrating to a reality more profound than its critics dream of, it justifies the designation 'romantic-realist', and the romantic-realist seeks that harmonizing beauty which is the essence of all things.

It is this religious instrument of the spirit, this experience of life, this vision of profound reality, this essential harmonizing beauty, that may be found, by those to whom they are of eternal value, in the novels and plays of Charles Morgan.

PART I

The World of the Novels and Plays

A world imaginatively comprehended; a spiritual and therefore miraculous world; a world that is significant rather than 'realistic'

THE TRADITION of realism in fiction, unknown to the Victorians, was established in this country early in the present century by Wells and Bennett and has held command of most of the field of the novel and the play for the last thirty years. Charles Morgan is not a realistic writer but an imaginative, if you like a romantic, one. He writes as an artist, whose aim is not realism but reality. Morgan tells us, through the mouth of Nigel Frew, how he conceives the artist's function and powers. An artist's work is more than a highly organized view of truth already accessible. He is not an interpreter of the common stock but a bringer of new truths. Art announces a transcendence, makes the walls of the world transparent. Art is news of reality not to be expressed in other terms. In this sense an artist is a messenger of the gods; the mind of the artist is creatively impregnated by the experience of his contact with the gods, and the making of the work of art is the harvesting of the original truth received. All perfect art is a likeness of God carved by himself in the sleep of the artist. The miracle ... declares itself.

Morgan would never have made these pretentious claims for himself, but in all his major works he writes with this power upon him, so that the vision of life that we get from him is of this transcendent order. The world of Charles Morgan derives its significance from being imaginatively conceived, and we must not ask that everything in it will bow to the demands of everyday probability. The episode of the £25,000 wager in *The Judge's Story* is quite fantastic and completely credible — on the imaginative level predicated, where disbelief is suspended. If Severidge is the Devil and Gaskony is the Good Man, nothing less than the offer of this huge sum for a book costing 8*s* 6*d* will suffice to show temptation triumphant, and only then because the good man is in a pit digged for him by others.

The imaginative approach perhaps finds its clearest manifestation in the contemplative ideal which, in one form or another, lies at the root of so many of Morgan's people: Nigel Frew, Lewis Alison, Narwitz, Sparkenbroke, Barbet Hazard, 'Heron', Judge Gaskony in his garret, probably David as a man, Ferrers with his mathematics, Christopher Terriford with his dream of the end of the era of power. And the practical result of the practice of contemplation is the building of the citadel of a tranquil soul. Lewis Alison is the chief exponent of the ideal, and 'Heron' shows the difficulty of its attainment in an age of violence.

Many of Morgan's characters have themselves the quality of creative imagination. And this not only with the confessed artists. It is imagination even more than love that enables Rydal to see the possibility of redemption in his dissolute wife. Marie Chassaigne's intuition was against believing 'Heron' guilty — but it was a diluted quality in her: she 'has not the grace to receive Grace'. In David's imagination Rose is a classical myth set to an English lyric. Barbet penetrates Thérèse's frivolous exterior to find a life-companion. Indeed it is in Barbet Hazard, wine-grower of the Charente and keeper of a comedy prison, that the creative force of imagination is most persuasively presented. When he wants something to happen, he instinctively imagines it happening, and if the operation of his mind is of the nature of a true imagining, of the kind, as Barbet puts it, that falls like the touch of a hand upon your shoulder (and he is always prepared for the possibility that what went on in his brain was just fancy, without creative consequence) — fulfilment is certain. His 'voyages', and the miracles we are coming to, are such imaginative fulfilments. And one cannot doubt that it was Barbet's 'imagining' of Thérèse that supported her and kept her true to herself and to him through her years of dissolute experience.

It is only in a world the essential stuff of which is not matter but spirit that imagination could function like this. Here 'the verb *to be* is eternal'; life *is*, and cannot be taken away. The apparent world is a cross-section of the inapprehensible yet ever-present world of immortality, and at a breath of vision the semi-opaque walls go down. In a world of this order, miracle — the happening that is not to be explained by laws of time and space — is accepted without surprise, 'a simple produce of the common day'. Barbet sees that he and Thérèse are part of a 'natural, and because natural miraculous, world'. Even Lancret, the priest, knows that 'miracles are more natural than what we call nature' — being due to 'a summoning of the reserves of nature'. But Barbet could have said with Whitman, 'As for me, I know of nothing else but miracles.' Cannock, in *The Empty Room*, on the other hand, voicing what he feels to be his unfitness to love Carey, says, 'I have become incapable of miracles, while hers are ahead of her.'

In most of the novels the action hinges at important moments on happenings of a questionable kind. The whole situation that constitutes the theme of *The Fountain* depends on the unlikely coming together — 'by what blessed chance!' — of Alison and Julie. When, in *The Judge's Story*, Gaskony had first met the woman of his life, by chance, in a book-shop, and she had handed over to him the book she was reading, the one he was in search of, *Marius the Epicurean*, he looked afterwards for 'an omen' on the page she had been reading — and found it there, clear and unmistakable. Sparkenbroke sees the hand of the gods in his early chance meetings with Mary, and presently each of these two can call the other into being by the exercise of imagination's power — or in Mary's case a prayer, 'O God, let him come!' In *The Voyage* and in *A Breeze of Morning* the truth and frequency of miracle are beautifully apparent. Barbet and Thérèse having missed the steamer on the Seine, it occurs to Thérèse that she will buy a boat, and as the thought enters her mind a boat puts off from the opposite bank — the man sails to where they are standing and turns out to be willing to sell. 'Why do you carry so much money, Thérèse?' Barbet asks, and she replies, 'To buy boats!'

Once, when Barbet is wandering over the vast complexities of Paris, seeking Thérèse, though he does not find her at once, he knows, 'Tonight I have been near her,' (and this was through a chance encounter with a boy and a cart) — and he thinks, 'if I had turned in suddenly at — but he could not see the turning; only the staircase, and the third landing ... ' — and when next morning she is found, his imagining was all true. The 'voyages' that are Barbet's most characteristic form of imaginative thought have a miraculous element, a 'voyage' being a sudden inspired breaking off from routine to do something quite different, to start a new kind of life. 'Death?' says Barbet — 'Yes, that would be a voyage, too.' His way with birds is not to be explained rationally, and there is the charming incident of the swallow trapped in the church. The one acclaimed miracle of Barbet's life, the quelling of the prison riot by non-resistance, was capable of a 'natural' explanation, and Barbet did not see it as miraculous: he says to his mother, 'If there was a miracle, it was not mine'; while Madame Hazard's own supernatural achievement, of seeing her son's escape from prison some days before it occurred, was perhaps a matter of telepathy.

In *A Breeze of Morning* — that most exquisite of all the novels — David Harbrook has complete faith in his 'magics', and uses them deliberately. The Letterby carriage is heard approaching, and not wishing to see Rose at that moment, David wills it into a grocer's cart. In a ball game on the lawn, wanting Rose not to miss a catch he has sent her, 'I prayed all the gods of Olympus to guide the ball into her hands. And the gods knew their own'. He wins his Eton scholarship through a miracle — by the Latin verses dictated to him by a power within him but not his own. And there are significant 'chance' happenings and 'coincidences', as when David, at a loose end, wanders on to the railway station and finds Rose about to ruin three — or four — lives by going to London for an elopement with Howard, and here now is David, able to carry the message of release and salvation.

Challenge to Venus presents an unusual case of miracles going wrong. Martin Lyghe is a 'plain man' with one exceptional imaginative feature, a faculty for getting sudden presentiments in which he goes into a kind of ecstasy and knows exactly what has to be done. Instances of this 'abrupt certainty' occurring before the opening of the tale are given, but it plays an ineffective part in the tale itself; in so far as these presentiments come to Martin they now prove false. The 'supernatural machinery' of this novel is seen rather in the sense experienced by everyone that Fiammetta is in danger by reason of her clear rivalling of the goddess, and there is a remarkable scene, pregnant with peril, where she deliberately matches her beauty against that of the Botticelli *Venus*. Fiammetta herself is scared: she feels guilty of 'an act of hubris — impiety'. And punishment falls at once.

The glory of Fiammetta is but one instance of the great over-riding miracle of beauty that shines in all the novels, most strikingly in *Portrait in a Mirror*, *The Fountain*, *Sparkenbroke*, *A Breeze of Morning*, and *Challenge to Venus*. Beauty — of nature and art, of the human spirit, and especially of woman — is the symbol of the divine in life, and it leads the heroes of these five novels like a star, perhaps sometimes misleads like a phantom. No novel can sink into the commonplace while the mystery of beauty is its inspiration.

In three more earth-bound novels glimpses of strange significance come through the mystery of human personality. In *The Judge's Story* the evil personality of Severidge is at war with sweetness and light in the persons of Gaskony and his ward, and the conflict, though played out on a purely human level, opens up to the imagination a suggestion of forces at work far below. In *The Empty Room* the love which does not alter when it finds alteration, and so redeems a bad — or perhaps merely weak and stupid — woman, produces an effect of something higher than human. And *The River Line*, both as play and as novel, gives in its closing scene an absorbing study of the interplay of human identity, where the personality of the dead man, 'Heron', practical yet contemplative, almost quietist but altogether sane, entering into the large and gentle spirit of Valerie, his half-sister, and energized and illuminated by the love between her and

Sturgess, gradually comes through to a knowledge of itself in a way that is psychologically intriguing and almost uncanny.

There are readers who are angrily antagonistic to the presentation of the world in this aspect, others, I suppose, who enjoy it but see it as playful, 'escapist'; the Morgan reader proper knows, either out of his own experience or through reading the authentic experiences of others, that the sense-world does not end with the senses but has a basis in the unknown, and that the familiar three-dimensional world is best explained as a cross-section of a four-dimensional spiritual reality. Such a reader will not only have no difficulty in accepting the non-realistic world of Charles Morgan but find it more interesting than the hard factual presentations of contemporary life that constitute the major part of modern fiction. Not, however, the whole of it. The element of strangeness in life, as represented in literature, suffered some discouragement from the mechanistic views of the later Nineteenth Century, but it has recently lifted its head again, and the aspect of Morgan's work considered in this chapter puts him into the company of Dunsany, Barrie, Conrad, Chesterton, James Stephens, E. M. Forster and J. B. Priestley.

A world in the main beautiful, good and happy; in which not evil but good predominates, both in human nature and in human destiny

ONE DOES not need to be a 'snob' to believe that beauty of the inner life, as well as of the not-to-be-despised outer, is achieved more readily in association with a certain degree of culture, and that this degree of culture is to some extent dependent on, though not today a concomitant of, a certain minimum of income. And though the social criticism expressed in the old farmer's generalization, 'The poor in a loomp is bad', no longer makes even the sense it may once have made, the later discovery enunciated by Eliza Doolittle that if you are rich it is easy to be at least clean and by implication good in other ways still contains a nucleus of truth. In short, the aesthetic and moral colour of a novelist's world will bear some relation to the social strata from which his characters are drawn. The factor of happiness is a more complex one, and bears no detectable relation to either income or social position, except that money takes the rough edge off some forms of misery.

With a few notable exceptions, Morgan's characters are taken from the English middle classes. Of exceptions 'above the line', we have Sparkenbroke, who is a hereditary peer, but so much more an artist that his social distinction is blurred, and samples of Dutch and Prussian aristocracy in *The Fountain*. 'Below the line' there are a rather greater but still unimportant number — boatmen, porters, a gentleman's gentleman, and so on. There are also French and Italians of mixed vintages, but by and large it is clear that what goodness, beauty and happiness we find in Morgan

23

will be such as are compatible with English middle-class life. The special temptations and stultifications of poverty are missing, we never come within sight of 'the criminal classes', there are always the guidance and standards provided by culture and breeding. In fact, there are no artificial obstacles to life being as good, beautiful and happy as it ought to be. The creator of this world has no predilection for sin and misery. He is an artist, and loves beauty, physical and moral, and its depiction.

For goodness, the world is not idyllic. In the first three novels, *Portrait in a Mirror*, *The Fountain* and *Sparkenbroke*, out of some twenty-five to thirty characters only two can be called 'bad' — Sophie van Leyden, who is jealous and spiteful, and Mary's father, Mr Leward, who is petty-minded and bad-tempered. Sparkenbroke is arguable — we shall return to him; and the betrayal of Narwitz by Alison and Julie will be better dealt with under the heading of 'morality'. Then come three novels in which 'badness' plays a larger part. In *The Voyage*, to balance the almost divine figure of Barbet Hazard, we have three profoundly evil characters, the vicious Blaquère, the insufferable Victor with his 'system' of spying and blackmail, and the base and greasy Templéraud. Thérèse, like Sparkenbroke, needs scrutiny. *The Empty Room* has for its situation the redemption of a woman who may be merely weak and stupid but in whom these equivocal qualities are so mingled with wilfulness and self-indulgence that the impression left on the mind is one of real 'badness'. In *The Judge's Story* Severidge is the very personification of evil — the Devil incarnate. After this we fall back to such moderate degrees of badness as the element of blind hate in old Chassaigne's patriotism, the small-minded obstructiveness of schoolmaster Libbett, and the unscrupulous machinations of the Admiral's wife in *The Flashing Stream*, this last figure showing plainly that Morgan understands the depths to which a woman can descend — within the class and cultural limits already indicated. Gerry Hardlip in *The Burning Glass* illustrates the new morality involved in the ideologies that have come to command the loyalties of so many men in the world of today.

To return to Sparkenbroke and Thérèse, two likeable people who obviously cannot be set up as saints. To the plain moralist — a somewhat rare person since 1914 — both are beyond the pale, Sparkenbroke because he is (we gather without actual observation) ready to seduce any number of women in order to obtain the 'release' which his artist's nature needs, Thérèse because she is promiscuous in her sex-relations. For his attitude to women I am prepared to condemn Sparkenbroke: human material is not to be consumed to satisfy even an artist's demands, and a rake with a theory is still a rake. But his depredations are a matter of the past: in the story before us, he is tempted to seduce Mary, but he recognizes her uniqueness and spares her, physically. He is as kind as he knows how to his wife, who continues to love and understand him, as does that grand fellow, George Hardy. All things considered, I am inclined to put Sparkenbroke with the sheep not the goats.

It should be clear by this time that when I label people 'good' or 'bad' I am not subjecting them to a moral code. To me a person is 'good' if he is kind and delightful, and his life and behaviour calculated to make his associates happy (Sparkenbroke does not answer up to this last requirement more than moderately). So with Thérèse: her promiscuity is shocking, her forcing of its details upon Barbet's unwilling ears even worse, but somehow she makes it appear a not very important aspect of her delightful personality. Barbet does not like it, but it does not make him stop loving her. Only at one point — in her passion for Templéraud (and it does not appear that Barbet knows about this) — does she go utterly and monstrously wrong, and we feel properly glad that she is brought sharply to her senses by quick and bitter disillusionment: she recovers our respect by taking her punishment like a man. At intervals throughout the book we get glimpses of an underlying and undeniable goodness, but her prime claim to virtue is that Barbet knows her through and through and yet entirely believes in her. She is transfigured in his company — exquisite, lovely, good, and one to whom miracles happen.

Of the positively 'good' people less need be said just now, though I cannot imagine a healthy-minded person failing to take delight in their company. I have already spoken of Barbet Hazard as the finest of all Morgan's male characters, as near to being Christ-like as a modern man may be, but entirely French and entirely without a mission. Henry Fullaton is in no way remarkable except in that his absence of jealousy, his single-souled recognition of the young genius who has suddenly come to outshine him, marks him out for pure goodness. George Hardy stands like the undimmed sun against the dubious moonlight morality of Sparkenbroke: he shares with Barbet Hazard a claim to be called a saint. Judge Gaskony has the final attribute of goodness, simplicity: like Tennyson's Great Duke he is 'in his simplicity sublime'. The calm sweet goodness of Ann Harbrook shines starlike over the desperate follies of Howard and Rose, and Benedetto in *Challenge to Venus* is one of God's own children. Narwitz creates an impression of supreme goodness, but this may be partly due to his capacity to endure suffering uncomplainingly. If there are readers to whom all this smacks of insipidity they should remember that Morgan is not the inventor of the purely good character: these people I have been describing were anticipated by those immortal creations, Henry Esmond, Mr Peggoty, Dorothea Casaubon, Gabriel Oak.

And does Morgan then (as was uncritically said of Wordsworth) ignore the fact of evil? In most of Morgan's novels and plays the atmosphere is charged with goodness, but evil is generally present as a minor disturbing element—a dangerous emotion in *Portrait in a Mirror, The Fountain, Sparkenbroke, A Breeze of Morning, Challenge to Venus*; a touch of fate in *The River Line*; evil-minded persons such as Blaquère, Victor Vincent, Templéraud, Lady Helston, Gerry Hardlip. But *The Judge's Story* seems to be deliberately written to show Morgan's appreciation of the power and nature of evil in the civilized world that is his province. The story shows good and evil evenly balanced, with evil only just failing to destroy good. In the modern world evil on a large scale can be exercised by an evil-minded person who has power in his hands either political or financial. Leaving political power alone, Morgan shows evil taking the form of a man of enormous wealth, acquired industrially, and powerful intellect, with a devilish determination to get certain good people (and in the last resort society as a whole) into his power and corrupt them. The man, George Severidge, is presented with every suggestion of Satanic personality, and his 'temptations', with their consequences and the resistance they provoke, constitute the substance of the novel.

Morgan pays due attention to evil, but is no specialist in the subject, as, according to Mr Graham Greene, Henry James was.* What Morgan understands and is interested in is that much more worth-while thing, goodness. I think he would have said that 'original sin' (that quaint conception to which so many people cling as to a cross) is an acceptable idea only if it is accompanied by a belief in original goodness. No, what Morgan does turn his eyes from is not evil but ugliness, and since modern literature, the theatre, the cinema, are overflowing with ugliness I am myself grateful to come to an oasis in the desert. There is suffering in his novels, but it is never squalid, and there is little of grossness in his bad people. I have pointed out that Severidge, the evillest person in the novels, is, like the Prince of Darkness, a gentleman, and it is all too easy, if you can keep your eyes off his cloven hoof, to fall into the mistake of finding him kind, well-meaning and attractive. A moralist with a delicate stomach might well be upset by Victor Vincent and Templéraud, and Venetia spilling whisky over the carpet and lying about it to her husband and herself is not a pretty sight. I find distasteful the spectacle of Nigel and Clare painfully working their sex-emotions up to sparking point. But the reader will have no difficulty in naming novelists one page from whom will shock the aesthetic nerves more violently than all these put together. And it is the same with suffering. There is a measurable degree of suffering in every one of Morgan's novels and plays, but only once, with Narwitz, is it

* 'Henry James understands evil better than anyone since Shakespeare' — a somewhat sweeping inference from *The Turn of the Screw*.

of a harrowing nature. There is one murder and one suicide, both done from the best of motives and with as little fuss as possible. I think there are only three other deaths, that of Narwitz, which was noble, that of Madame Hazard, which was natural, and that of Sparkenbroke, which brought peace to three disturbed spirits. The Crime Club addict finds all this *very* tame.

There are good and evil in human nature, and there are good and evil in human fate, in the lives of men and women; and he would be a wise man who could demonstrate with certainty the interdependence, or inter-relation, of the one species of good and evil and the other. In the novels and plays of Charles Morgan the relation is clearer and more ideal. On the whole the 'bad' people suffer and are unhappy, the 'good' prosper, or are at least happy. There are exceptions. So far as we can see, the detestable Templéraud goes successfully and smoothly on his lying way, and Victor Vincent, though defrauded of his expected victim, Barbet, will probably continue to work his 'system' without disaster or further failure. On the other side, there is the shocking treatment of Narwitz, and the 'execution' that brought incredulity into 'Heron's' eyes. Poor Benedetto, who is nothing short of a saint, is left miserable and hopeless at the end of Fiammetta's story. But more often the nice people come into their own. George and Mary Hardy have been helpless in the grip of a force neither can control, but they have each recognized salvation in the other, and when Mary has come back, having wandered within an inch of destruction, George, looking down on her sleeping, sighing form, knows she has chosen happiness. The ending of *The Voyage* is as exquisitely peaceful as that of *Paradise Lost*, only Barbet, who has always been as happy as he is good, and Thérèse, who has at least been thrillingly alive, have found, not lost, their paradise. Judge Gaskony, not of his own intention but through the machinations of his devilish enemy, achieves the one condition in which he can carry undistractedly on with his *Athenian*, in the knowledge that Vivien too is now safe from further temptation and about to start on a happy 'voyage' with her Henry. And in what lovely tranquillity does Ann Harbrook's story end as she looks back 'happily and silently over the long memories'.

Thus deliberately does Morgan apportion destinies, and again it seems to me that experience shows something like this fair treatment in the lives of actual men and women. In youth one dreams of a just world; presently one is raging at the indecencies of fate; but after many years — years that may or may not have brought 'the philosophic mind', but at least years of observation both wide and close — one seems to see the distribution of blows and favours as having a certain reasonableness.

Happiness is not synonymous with good fortune, and is not always the result of either being fortunate or doing good, though it has a closer connection with beauty. Happiness does not come out of experience, but out of the self, and moulds experience. With Morgan happiness in individuals is much involved with a quality to be discussed later — tranquillity or (to use Morgan's own word) invulnerability. This quality lies at the base of such characters as Lewis Alison, George Hardy, Barbet Hazard, Judge Gaskony, Valerie Barton, Karen Selby, while its achievement is the Sangraal of Sparkenbroke's lifelong quest. Only George Hardy and Barbet possess their souls thus completely.

There are few positively unhappy people in Morgan, but in one of them, Lancret the priest in *The Voyage*, Morgan shows a complete understanding of unhappiness. Significantly enough, Lancret is the only character to feel that sense of sin which, according to one brand of Churchmanship, is essential to the soul's health and characteristic of high religious natures. Julie in *The Fountain* is oppressed by the knowledge of what she is doing to her husband, Philip Sturgess by the thought that he had set in motion the process which led to the killing of 'Heron', but in neither case is the feeling one of having sinned against God. In fact religion, a relation with God and a recognition of God's law, is almost entirely lacking from the world depicted by Morgan. Rector Hardy's interests lie more in Latin verse than in Hebrew scripture, and his admiration for Sparkenbroke as a poet quite submerges any disapprobation he may have felt for

29

his morals. Barbet says his prayers before getting into bed, and
Fiammetta is a devout Catholic, yet neither in Barbet's blessedness nor in Fiammetta's passions do we feel that religion plays any
part, helpful or restraining. Christopher Terriford's objection to
the use of the power that lies in his Burning-glass is not that it is
un-Christian (he is willing that it should be used to destroy his
country's enemies) but that power for power's sake, and more and
more of it, is an evil thing, corrupting the mind of man. Lewis
Alison argues almost as a Christian against Narwitz's pagan
philosophy, but he expressly denies holding faith in Christian
doctrine. The one man whose outlook has some semblance of
being religious (in a non-theological sense) is Sparkenbroke,
whose imaginative understanding of an infinite life beyond the
sense, to which the ultimate entry is afforded by death, even
literally by the 'tomb', represents, if in unorthodox terms, one
of the elements in the Christian philosophy. It is clear that
Morgan has chosen to present a world where religion and its
sanctions have even less effect on the thoughts and conduct of its
inhabitants than they have in the 'real' world.

Finally, the world that Morgan constructs for us is a beautiful
world (and this may rouse less opposition), not only, as we have
seen, avoiding ugliness but built of material that must delight
the aesthetic sensibilities in innumerable ways. The motive of
each novel is generally a conception of great spiritual beauty.
Such are Nigel Frew's passion of painting, Lewis Alison's contemplative dream, diverted but not destroyed by violent love,
Sparkenbroke's philosophy of art, love and death, with George
Hardy's quiet and patient but no less creative way of life, Barbet's
lovely soul and his theory of voyages, Judge Gaskony's unaggressive integrity, the morning freshness of David Harbrook's
worship of his goddess, the vision of Fiammetta appearing in her
Psyche's niche to challenge Aphrodite and pay for her audacity ...
The spirit is clarified, the heart is uplifted, the eyes rejoice at the
spectacle of these several microcosms all so different but all
glowing with the light of beauty.

Every novel and play, apart from its large conceptual beauty, contains some memorable element of peculiar charm. In *The Judge's Story* the utter trust and intimacy of the Gaskony brothers, so simple, sweet and sincere, is of this kind, while we can also delight in the thought of that poor lodging in Cliftonville in which the Judge, struck down but unharmed, finds salvation — 'infinite riches in a little room'. Until the suspicion of treachery comes to shatter the dream, the fascination of the passengers down the 'river line' by the personality and outlook of their tall bird-like companion is a theme of tranquillity in the turmoil of danger, and later the theme is revived in the person of his sister Valerie. In *A Breeze of Morning* we have a heart-warming picture of David's home life with his exceptionally human father and the exquisite Ann, while both in this book and in *Sparkenbroke* there are chapters in which a passage of classical poetry is expounded, in one case by Squire Letterby, that self-confessed ancient Roman, and in the other by Rector Hardy, in a way to give pure and lasting delight. Every scene between Barbet and Thérèse is as beautiful as a flowering shrub, and a peculiar beauty attaches to the frequent pictures we are given of Madeleine and her relations with Cugnot. There are interiors that glow with a warm bright-ness in the home occupied by the Hardy family and in that — in spite of melodramatic irruptions — of Christopher and Mary Terriford. And beyond all this, at the heart of each novel is a girl or woman of extreme physical beauty. This is not the moment for scrutinizing them but I look forward to an opportunity of doing so later.

Morgan has chosen to select (all art being based on selection) from the living scene mainly people who are good and beautiful beyond the common run, though not beyond what Humbert Wolfe called 'the uncommon man and woman', and I for one am more grateful to him than to some other novelists whose preferences lead them to overload their stage with figures whose depravity makes one hot and whose appearance leaves one cold. He writes in the spirit of poetry, depicting the drama of life not as the contem-porary eye sees it but as he himself tentatively understands it, or guesses at its essential truth, in the light of eternity. In this light it may well appear a better and more beautiful world than as photographed upon the jaundiced eye of a disgruntled observer. Morgan is a writer of high seriousness but not a tragic writer. There is conflict, but it is resolved, there is suffering, but it is compensated. He was not without experience of intense suffering himself, but it did not cloud his vision or embitter his spirit. The lasting impression left by the world of his creation is one of truth and beauty.

CHAPTER THREE

A world in which love is either sacred or profane

IN THE three novels which constitute what I call 'the *Sparkenbroke* trilogy' the action has a twin-engine motive, love and art, the action really arising out of the interplay of these two. The 'love' is a physical ecstasy, an irresistible urge to copulate. Desire may appear to those who desire to be the bearer of a more than physical message, but under whatever aspect, the supreme good, or this one of the two supreme goods, is what is picturesquely called 'the bliss of nakedness'. The other supreme good, which makes it possible for this kind of love to be regarded as having a spiritual significance, is the passion of art, philosophy or poetry. *Portrait in a Mirror* begins as a representation of the mystery of art and the nature of the artist and ends as a study of lust. In *The Fountain* even the dream of the contemplative life breaks up temporarily under the pressure of sex-impulse. Sparkenbroke attempts to dignify the sex-act as a means of giving him release for the purposes of poetry, but whatever its secondary function he pursues its primary one as assiduously as any debauchee (has at least done so before the book opens).

Then it appears that Morgan realized that he had played variations enough on this theme. He took up a motif that had already sounded in the earlier compositions and made it one of the subjects (in the musical sense) of the next four novels as well as of the plays, involving with it a greater variety of character and plot than the first three novels had exhibited. The motif was that of a quieter, more controlled, less primitive love. There had been glimpses of this in *The Fountain*. One was afforded by the singularly attractive figure of 'Elizabeth', to whom Alison had been engaged before he got lost in Holland under war conditions; we see her but shadowily, through his mother's letters, but I feel she might have fitted in better than Julie with Alison's ideal of the inviolable citadel of inward peace. The other glimpse came through Alison's prison-companion, Ramsdell, with his pointed rejoinder to Julie, 'More than the romantics suppose, love is a thing one permits or denies to oneself.' And of course the secondary theme of *Sparkenbroke*, George Hardy's love for Mary — and hers for him, was entirely in this key.

And now this quieter love, intense but not feverish, less spectacular but made to last, becomes, in the person of Barbet Hazard, one of the major themes of *The Voyage*. In writing about Browning, whose love-poetry is, more than that of any other poet, inspired by this kind of love, I called it 'true' love as opposed to the 'romantic' love which is the source of most erotic literature in verse or prose. Ramsdell, above, uses the word 'romantic' in my sense, which does not generally connote marriage. Alison and Julie are indeed expecting to marry on their return to England, now that Narwitz is dead, but Julie at least is aware that their love is not necessarily, not yet proved to be, of the stuff that endures. Barbet, on the other hand, who I have suggested exemplifies a 'true' and enduring love, has no plan for marrying Thérèse when they set out, at the end of the book, on their ultimate 'voyage', yet I feel that this voyage is going to be a long one, that they will make it side by side, and that they will be married in spirit if not in law.

Now I am not saying that the four novels that followed *Sparkenbroke* — *The Voyage*, *The Empty Room*, *The Judge's Story* and *The River Line* — all carry on the theme of 'true' love, the love that is the privilege of George Hardy and Barbet Hazard. I don't know that it makes its appearance at all after *The Voyage*. But 'romantic' love is relegated to minor issues. It appears in the innumerable affairs of Thérèse, is emphatically 'profane' in that with Templéraud, and characterizes the abortive entanglement of Howard and Rose in *A Breeze of Morning*.

I have suggested above that the criterion of 'true' love is that it leads to marriage or the desire for it, but this does not mean that marriage is always or often founded on 'true' love. There are studies of the married condition in Sparkenbroke and Lady Sparkenbroke, George and Mary, Rydal and Venetia, Henry and Vivien, Julian and Marie, Christopher and Mary Terriford, and a few slighter sketches. The Sparkenbroke marriage is pathetically uneasy, and is only maintained as a going concern by reason of decent kindness on Sparkenbroke's part, love and tolerance on Lady Sparkenbroke's part, good breeding on both sides, and their joint interest in the child. George Hardy's marriage is likely to be happy, now that Sparkenbroke is out of the way, but it is obviously not ideal. The 'true' love, passionate without being out of control, is on George's side, as is safest, and Mary will love him tenderly, but not with an equal love — after all, she is only half his age. Morgan makes a point of there being considerable discrepancy of age between the lovers in his novels, but other than George and Mary the married couples are evenly matched in this respect. The marriage of Henry and Vivien has the unimpassioned beauty that forms the basis of most successful marriages. There are signs that love goes much deeper with Christopher and Mary Terriford in *The Burning Glass*. But in all these cases the marriage situation is a background element in a story where the primary interest is all-absorbing.

It is worthy of note that Morgan allows some of his most attractive girls and women to marry, and remain comfortably married, on mere liking, having found, or being destined to find, love elsewhere: so with Clare in *The Portrait*, Rose in *A Breeze of Morning*, Marie in *The River Line*, and probably Fiammetta in *Challenge to Venus* (for we gather she will marry Rinaldo, the Black Ram of Benedetto's aversion). I have heard women question the likelihood of Marie Chassaigne's being able to accept in marriage the man who had killed the man she had really loved. But they were companions in distress — Julian had killed 'Heron' on Marie's order. Moreover, 'Heron' had not returned Marie's love, and the French view of marriage is said to lack the romantic flavour English people like to find in it. A similar and perhaps even greater obstacle lay between Philip Sturgess and 'Heron's' sister Valerie (as Sturgess was only too painfully aware), and Morgan stresses the unusual quality in Valerie that enabled her to surmount the obstacle. But some writers would have dealt more fully with the psychological problems involved in these two cases, and the truth is that Morgan is not interested in marriage. The loveliest pictures he gives of 'true' love result in actual marriage only in one instance, that of George Hardy, where the 'form' of the marriage is so perfect that it is felt to be — to use Morgan's favourite word—invulnerable. The completeness with which this marriage and that in *The Burning Glass* are visualized shows that my assertion that Morgan is not interested in marriage needs qualification, more of which comes from the rather odd and obscure story of the erring wife and the magnanimous husband in *The Empty Room*. Nevertheless it is true to say that he puts his most concentrated power, his most acute analysis, into his studies of flaming romantic passion. He is perhaps of Santayana's opinion: 'It takes patience to appreciate domestic bliss: volatile spirits prefer unhappiness.'

When I turn again to the 'true' love of Barbet for Thérèse— so tender, unaltering, understanding and undemanding — and after much turmoil, hers for Barbet, I am at a loss to know whether to call it married love or not. Certainly Barbet says to Thérèse, 'Perhaps I don't love you as men love women who share their lives', and towards the end Thérèse reflects that domestic happiness is not the right end to all love stories: 'I am I and he is he ... and we are on separate voyages.' But Morgan's own comment on her is that she 'wished that a romantically domestic scene might be given her to play in her own life', and the concluding words of the tale show Barbet with a tranquil mind based perhaps partly on faith in his miracles.

Strangely enough, the other two people in *The Voyage* who offer some evidence of being in a state of 'true' love are also not married, Cugnot and Madeleine, between whom there is a relationship completely different in kind from that of Thérèse with Templéraud and not much more like that of Thérèse with

Barbet. The bond between Cugnot and Madeleine is immaterial but strong, like the gossamer shackles that bound Fenrir the Wolf. He knows that freedom is there, and defines freedom as 'being able to walk out of this room and not to feel that I have to return — not to feel that I am on a piece of elastic that will make me want to come back'. But he admits that he is incapable of accepting this freedom — 'I need you to look after me': an excuse I suppose many a man has made for continuing to love his wife. It was Cugnot's habit to neglect Madeleine, to treat her, when it pleased him, as if she did not exist, 'and it was her power over him that she could without resentment and, indeed, with a unique pride, be neglected'. Marriages have been wrecked on the wife's not unreasonable refusal to share Madeleine's spirit of acceptance. The irregular union doubtless owes its success to the fact that both the parties to it are delightful people, and many a happy marriage depends on nothing more specific than this. One may round off the list of situations in Morgan that are marriages in spirit with a mention of Will Gaskony's lasting and effectual, romantic yet 'true', love for his lost Julia.

Nevertheless it must again be admitted that Morgan devotes his most interested attention to the depiction of love outside marriage, and when we remember that his great predecessor in the novel of love, Hardy, has a number of profound studies of the married situation we may be forced to the conclusion that in Morgan we see a relapse to the older Victorian principle that when a love-story had been brought to the moment of marriage it was time for the book to end. And, leaving marriage — a convention — aside, I feel that Morgan has nowhere shown an understanding of a love, sacred and profane, romantic and true, passionate, immortal, and not wholly dependent on primitive sex, such as is seen in the love of Hardy's Jude and Sue or that of Cathy and Heathcliff in *Wuthering Heights*.

Outside the '*Sparkenbroke* trilogy' and the last of the novels, where they play a too obsessive part, Morgan shows love and sex forming one among other worth-while interests and activities. This, I believe, is the part they play in the lives of most people, and we may conclude that in this matter Morgan's world is more realistic than in some others. It is pleasant to note that in the last marriage situation he imagined, that of Christopher and Mary Terriford in *The Burning Glass*, we have the one marriage that can be called perfect — a marriage not only ideal but 'real'.

CHAPTER FOUR

A world predominantly intellectual

PERHAPS THE respect in which Morgan's world differs most widely from the workaday one is in the ratio of intellectual people to the other kind. Iago, speaking in days before the helicopter, said that most people were as well fitted for thinking as for flying, and sad experience bears him out. Goodness and kindness in plenty, and intelligence in fair supply, but of intellect little sign. Outside carefully chosen circles, few people can put two consecutive thoughts together, or distinguish a plain fallacy from a vital truth, or see any fact whatsoever in its proper light and relation. As for conducting or following a logical argument, the ability to do this is not much more common than the ability to run a mile in four minutes. Yet all these things (apart from the running) are done constantly and as a matter of course by most of Morgan's characters. As we noted in another connection, it is not that Morgan sees society like this, but that he chooses to select, to the end of enjoyable writing and reading, men and women whose conversation has method and substance. He does not wish to compose, and we do not have to read, records of the inane dialogue of which some other novels so 'realistically' consist. A rapid survey of the novels and plays from this angle will prove, if proof were needed, my point.

In *Portrait in a Mirror* Nigel Frew, though but a seventeen-year-old ex-schoolboy, has arrived at complete theories of the art of portraiture. He says, and says with authority, 'Painting is a contemplative as well as an executive act. To paint a portrait is to discover the springs of a life; to know by what courses the streams come down from the hills of childhood ... perhaps to guess a little of the seas to which they go.' And his observations on life outside his art contain what might seem to be the wisdom

39

of experience: 'To show her (the ancient lady, Miss Fullaton) as she was — unashamed but not shameless; to exhibit in her that rare product of worldliness — a cynic who is not a spiritual dullard ... ' It is unlikely, but it makes for worth-while reading. The action of the *Portrait* is not constructed of intellect but of desperate emotions, yet it is carried on among people who have brains. Doggin, the art teacher, is a philosopher as well; and there are Agatha Trobey and Great-aunt Fullaton, both of whom can converse with Nigel at his own level.

On the other side, Henry Fullaton and his son Ned are simple souls who do not aspire to do more than scratch about — Ned surlily, his father contentedly — on the surface of things, while Nigel's parents are just plain dumb. As for Clare herself, she has a mind of better quality than those of the other two Morgan women whose beauty is depicted as dangerous, Rose and Fiammetta, but it is not good enough to show her the folly of pressing on to its disastrous end the sordid sex-passion she has conceived for Nigel.

The Fountain is massively intellectual, only Julia's Dutch step-relatives being represented as dim-witted, with the exception of the Baron, who has the profound wisdom of the soil. Julie herself is not intimidated by her two philosopher lovers, Alison and Narwitz, and Alison's companion officers are mostly capable of clear thinking. Herriott, for instance, understands Alison's quest for peace, and puts forward the suggestion that he is of the kind to find stillness, or the meaning of life, not in solitude but in the world. So with the next novel: Sparkenbroke himself, George Hardy and the Rector are all men of strong intellect; Helen, George's sister, shares the family brains, and Lady Sparkenbroke is not so far beneath her brilliant husband in mind as she is above him in morals, though her inability to understand why, as a boy, he was attracted by the tomb in the mound is a measure of her limitations. Sparkenbroke's philosophy is an aesthetic one, but it is intellectually held and supported by argument. Even his man, Bisset, has more brain than is strictly necessary for a valet: he can keep up a few exchanges with his master without discomfort. As for Mary, she would have been fearfully wasted on Peter, the tale's one oaf. Though but eighteen, she penetrates to the heart of Sparkenbroke's poetry so keenly that she is able to suggest to him the transitional passage which he cannot find himself, between the two parts of his story of Nicodemus. Her conversations with George always proceed on lines of sweet reasonableness, in contrast with the erotic mysticism that sometimes falsifies her exchanges with Sparkenbroke.

Thus, in the 'trilogy', there has been but a meagre handful, four or five in all, of characters to represent the general low intellectual level of human society, against a large company any of whom would stand out in a room of educated people. *The Voyage* breaks this habit, as we have found it doing in other ways, at least to the extent of there being a fifty-fifty ratio of dullards. All the Vincent family — Emilie and her three children, Bette, Pierre and even Victor with his spider-web; Madame Hazard and her elder son Anton, both of whom have indeed a quality that removes them from the class of stupid without putting them among the intellectuals; Templéraud and Annette — all these are mentally commonplace. And yet in another way this novel keeps up the Morgan way of an impossibly high intellectual standard. Regard Thérèse: a village girl, illegitimate daughter of a country priest and of a woman of whom we know nothing except that she went in to cook and clean for him and had pretty ears; a *diseuse*, graduating from a rustic inn to the neighbouring town and thence by stages to Paris, where she increases her professional earnings by lavish prostitution. Yet the girl, from first to last, never makes a pointless remark or utters a sentiment that is not full of logical content clearly conceived. Among her lovers is Philippe Courcelet, an intellectual of the first water and one of the most influential diplomats in Paris: he finds Thérèse's conversation continuously stimulating, and she has no difficulty in conducting with him long abstruse arguments on history, morals and affairs generally. The parallel with Aspasia and Pericles is obvious (with the substitution of a vine-grower for the cattle-dealer!), but Aspasia had advantages of birth and education denied to Thérèse (though of course the priest doubtless played his part in her heredity). It is all made convincing by the consistency with which the whole personality of the girl is drawn, so that we feel it is impossible that such a girl should have lacked a vigorous mind. She is made to think deeply as well as talk brilliantly, and sometimes her self-communings, her analyses of her position, her intentions and her state of mind are extended wearisomely, but there are few philosophers of whom this could not be said. And her thoughts are full of interest. She reflects on her second profession, and explains to Courcelet, 'Men are so easy to deceive that it seems a waste of time to be true to them. They don't really appreciate it. They don't know the difference'; or again, 'Perhaps I should say "so far as I am capable of allowing any man to love me". Oh, that wouldn't be true if the man were my equal or if he were *more* than I am, but no man ever is. They are all like actors who don't know their parts. I have to carry the scene — I have to; it's true; they are so little.' She can analyse Courcelet: 'He is clever, my poor Philippe, Thérèse thought, there is point in everything he says, but it takes you no further. What he said then is true — perhaps it is true — it seemed true and I remember it, but though it sounds like an answer it is, like the answers of all clever men, only the question repeated.' She can learn from Barbet: reading his letters, 'she, who had believed a loving covetousness to be a sign and part of love itself, saw for the first time that there was an alternative to it that was not indifference—a fullness of recognition, a calm and passionate acceptance of unity within the ultimate unity of all sentient creatures'.

For Barbet himself, it would be a misuse of words to call him an intellectual, but he is of that greater species, the poets, arriving at a more than intellectual truth by intuition, that is, by simply being his simple self (the 'self' being of a certain quality) and seeing things without inhibition, fear, prejudice or the warping of false learning or personal desire. He is never humiliated because he never tries to be other than what he solidly is, and as such he is any man's equal. On his first visit to Paris in search of Thérèse he wanders into the Ecurie Plence and finds himself surrounded by a brilliant selection of Parisian artists, men and women, who would undoubtedly, if he had been the simpleton he might seem, have driven the intruder out of their club by laughter and scorn. But Barbet is instantly and un-self-consciously at his ease and accepted as one of them, and he presently makes them listen to him and take his word for Thérèse and her excellence. And on a second visit, there are new men there who begin to bait him, but Barbet smilingly stands his ground and puts them down one by one. There is only one parallel — the quiet confident unexpected answers by which Christ silenced his attackers. Barbet and Thérèse provide the only signs that Morgan understood the claims of democracy, but they are enough to substantiate those claims.

Courcelet is Barbet's antithesis, pure intellect entirely lacking the divine spark; Lancret the erring priest is intellect gone dark and sour; Cugnot and Madeleine, as a pair, represent sweetness and light; Plence is the impresario with a mind. *The Voyage* is indeed the third of another trilogy, three books which, to be fully appreciated, demand a good deal of mental concentration.

In *The Empty Room* most of the characters are at least educated, but there is not more of intellect in this slight novel than there is of anything else. With *The Judge's Story* we rise to greatness again, and though the action has elements of melodrama it has an intellectual basis in the conflict of good and evil, and it is played out entirely by intellectuals, though their intellect sits lightly on them. Will Gaskony is a retired judge and his brother Dick head of an Oxford college. We have not to assume that Severidge's millions required a high order of intellect to make, but in his relations with Gaskony and the others he does show just that combination of quick brain and absence of moral scruple that is supposed to mark big business. Gaskony's ward, Vivien, on the other hand, has not only a keen mind but goodness to match. Her husband, young Henry Lerrick, has brains enough to work out Severidge's world-scheme for him but has to be told by his wife to what disastrous ends it will lead. The last chapters, where Gaskony saves Vivien's soul through Milton and Plato, give the story its stamp.

A Breeze of Morning, that seemingly light but really profound novel, is peopled almost entirely by characters who use their brains to good effect. The 'odd man out' is Rose, whose creator has taken good care that her divine loveliness shall not be marred by what Hardy calls the fine destructive lines of thought. Beauty's self, and of an infinite charm, she is deliberately shown as slow-witted. To the Seafords she is just a girl who chatters and eats chocolate biscuits, and even the worshipping David glimpses her mental limitations. She is, in short, so far as her mind goes, a suitable match for Dick Featherford, the other non-intellectual of the story. David, though a boy, has a clear and efficient brain polished by his study of Greek and Latin and is earmarked for a First at the University. His father, an eminent engineer, gives quiet signs of the powerful mind his profession requires, and his daughter Ann is carved from the same block as David. Then there is Squire Letterby, whose training of David in classics gives spirit to the lifeless knowledge acquired at school.

It would be doing a disservice to the warm-hearted Italian world of *Challenge to Venus* to call it intellectual, yet, apart from Fiammetta herself, not only the subtle aristocrat, Count Ascanio, as brilliant a talker as Courcelet, but all the Varenese we meet, seemingly so deliciously naïve, think and speak with clarity and penetration, though Benedetto's heart moves on lines of such pure goodness of feeling that there is not room in his mind for the exercise of the logic that denies. Sullivan is an ex-Oxford tutor, and Martin Lyghe, once his pupil, has a good brain, though it allows him to slip into the absurdity of supposing he can argue Fiammetta into an English marriage. Nearly all the characters in the three plays are intellectuals.

The problems that arise to disturb the lives of Morgan's people are due to the tensions set up by vagaries of emotion and passion, but, except in *Portrait in a Mirror*, these problems are generally solved by intellectual processes. What brings Alison and Julie together is something entirely emotional, but the coming and death of Narwitz sets reason working, and at the end of the novel they are both engaged on that praiseworthy business, thinking out how best to adapt the rest of life to the new conditions. Sparkenbroke's relations with Mary are quite remarkably under the rule of his mind and will, and though Mary is at the mercy of the current of romantic passion, it is George's deep but rational feeling that ultimately takes charge. Barbet and Thérèse keep a firm grip on the reins of love till they are both completely 'ready' and 'know what to do'. Judge Gaskony evades Severidge's toils by the plainest exercise of wisdom. Rose uses common sense to decide between a silly elopement with Howard and a prosaic marriage with Matho. The plays are all studies in the rational approach to problems of various kinds, intellectual tinged with passion in *The Flashing Stream*, in *The River Line* self-preservation and psychological obstacles to love, in *The Burning Glass* the question of life's greatest good. It is all an aspect of Morgan's deliberate choice of people of high quality for his *dramatis personae*.

Thackeray accepted the world as he found it; Morgan refuses to do this. So we get from him an improbable world, an idealized world, a poet's world: but, I contend, a perfectly fascinating world to anyone who enjoys intellectual society and the sight of cultured men and women pitting their brains against the challenge offered by an unpredictable universe.

PART II

The Art of the Novels and Plays

CHAPTER ONE

Action

Ars est celare artem. Well, is it? The unfathered dictum (and merely Latin at that) implies that 'art' is something to be ashamed of instead of the correlative and instrument of genius. It is not to be obtruded, or to produce a sense of effort, but if we can feel, as we regard a creative work, not only how beautiful that is but how beautifully that is done, it seems to me we should get an added pleasure. Are not the openings of *Twelfth Night, Paradise Lost, Hyperion, Zuleika Dobson* nicely contrived to give the maximum of delight, and can we, do we, object?

I have to confess that I derive an almost continuous satisfaction from observing the admirable artistic power with which Morgan consciously fashions his material, both in the mass and at every point of detail. Consider for example that matter of opening chapters or situations. (And I know, as Shakespeare did, that a brilliant beginning is much easier to come by than a satisfying ending: we shall look at Morgan's endings later.) *Portrait in a Mirror* opens quietly, plainly, almost timidly compared with what was to come in the next book; but how effective is that picture of the young hero's home at 'Drufford in Kent', with its mid-Victorian parents coming down hard if kindly on Nigel's twenty-three-year-old sister, crushing incipient rebellion by a lovingly intended piece of bitter humiliation; the elder brother with his intriguing account of the young woman — 'deuced pretty' but emotional and flirtatious — with whom Nigel was presently to fall in love; and Nigel himself, eighteen but called a 'little idiot' by his sister when he goes to her bedroom to offer sympathy. A bright and realistic introduction to a story that passes almost immediately into coloured realms of fantasy. When, more than twenty years later, Morgan wrote, in *A Breeze of*

D

Morning, another version of the same story, his art had developed to the point where he could begin at the end, giving us, in his first chapter, the reflections of the even more youthful hero, now in middle age, on what had been, and so enabling us to estimate the quality of the boyish mind that could distinguish between the mask and the face and perceive in the empty-headed Rose Letterby the very divinity of beauty. And then the beginning proper — the 'luminous moment' of leaving the school building, followed by the matter-of-fact description of the coaching that was just over and the road home that was being taken by the imaginative boy for whom the rooks left lines of silver as they flew and Mr Crutwell walking in front of him had someone else's face; and then the almost forbidden path through the park which he takes with a sense that something may be going to happen — as indeed something tremendous did.

The opening chapter of *The Fountain* is famous, with its picture, painted with Dutch fidelity, of the carriageful of officers going into internment:

> On an afternoon of January 1915, a small train dragged itself across the flat Dutch countryside in the neighbourhood of Bodegraven, carrying a group of English officers under guard. Their heads appeared continually at the windows, for, though their destination had been kept from them, they judged by a restless movement of the guard that they were near the end of their journey.

Most of the men are suggested in flashes of dialogue, but a full-length portrait is offered at once of Lewis Alison, a dark, craggy man of more than common height, with vigour and eagerness in his eyes and something austere and disciplined in his expression. The core of his personality is given: 'a composure not easily to be disturbed', a passionately held conception of 'a struggle for some kind of stillness within oneself' — together with hints of the conflicting passion that is to trouble his ideal, memories of a girl whom he had once tutored and who is now living at the castle at Enkendaal. The chapter is not only fascinating in its realistic detail, but so significantly informative that a reader with the necessary talent could construct in outline the story that is to follow — all except its most original element, the entry and impact of Narwitz.

Sparkenbroke, alone among the novels, has a prologue, an event happening twenty years before the story proper begins. Its first chapter is a brilliant evocation of the idea of 'the Sparkenbroke mound' and its symbolization of death as an entry into the reality from which the life of the senses is an exile: the scene of the book's end. We move about in time, seeing Piers Sparkenbroke now as a boy of twelve, now — by way of the inscription on the tomb—as the poet he became. We are avid to know more about this Mound, and about Sparkenbroke as boy and man. With the opening of *The Voyage* we are plumb at the centre of the story — Barbet himself: 'Standing on a ladder propped against the white walls of the house Barbet was re-painting the shutters of the Maison Hazard.' How characteristic — Barbet, master of the establishment but with no sense of his own importance, chaffing his mother and singing small songs to keep time with his brush. Then an accurate plan of the old house and the prison it includes with the distillery, and half Barbet's character and story in the sentence that concludes the opening section:

> When responsibility for the little prison came to Barbet, he disliked it, for he did not see himself as a warder of men, but he discharged it as well as he could and, since he might not release his prisoners, made friends with them.

The Empty Room begins in a war atmosphere, but without the personal urgency of the opening of *The Fountain*. Moreover, the actual opening sentence, 'On the first Sunday in November, the third month of the war, Richard Cannock performed, on a woman's eye, a bold and subtle operation that gave him the satisfaction a writer may have in a flawless paragraph', creates a very unusual impression of effect deliberately sought. How different when we turn to the next novel, *The Judge's Story*. The book opens with a picture of George Severidge, a precise, economical and unlaboured account, fascinating and humorous, of his methodical habits, neutral in impression till we discover, at the end of the second paragraph, his cynical attitude to women and people in general, and we know what kind of man it is who now meets the elderly, boyish, innocent retired Judge. There are hints that Severidge is, in some sense, the Devil, and it is obvious that he is out to lay temptation in the Judge's way. As with *The Fountain*, the story is implicit in the first chapter.

The River Line is a book in which the history of past events is gradually unfolded, and we are at once set wondering about Philip Sturgess, who has come from America with certain specific inquiries in view: he has to find out about Julian and Marie whom he is to meet again after a long-since parting in France; and especially about Marie, who has suffered terribly in a German camp. The opening paragraph is worth reproducing:

> As his train from London approached Kemble, only the impassivity of his English fellow-passengers kept Sturgess silent. This was the last stage of a long journey from America, and what he would find at the end of it had been the principal reason for his having come. He wanted to rejoice with someone. Happily expectant, he would have liked to express his happiness in friendly talk — with anyone, about almost anything. Instead, he smiled to himself and said nothing.

Sturgess's part in the River Line episode, his remorse and redemption, are the theme of the book, and his happy open personality runs like a golden thread through the highly wrought material of the story. Yet this colourful opening is less revealing than some others, since it gives no sign of Sturgess's torn conscience. (The *River Line* play begins later in the story, and apparently less effectively, but a play has great auxiliaries, in the stage-setting and the actors, which can create the atmosphere for which the novel depends purely on words.)

'The bed was too small for him, but he was accustomed to that.' This abrupt first sentence of *Challenge to Venus* is the beginning of a sequence of paragraphs that deal entirely with Martin Lyghe's splendid physical endowment, including his 'fiery' though now darkened red hair, and this is proper, since the book is to be about a sex-attraction which is wholly physical on both sides. This and the rich Italian scene are the notes struck in the overture, with a clear suggestion of the Aghinolfi theme, and a bare hint of something queer in Martin's mental make-up.

Each of the openings described is beautifully calculated to catch our interest and make us realize there is a fascinating story to come: it is like meeting a stranger who we instantly know is going to start a new chapter in our life. From the openings we learn too what kind of novel it is that Morgan writes. The Morgan novel is a novel of character and situation, of character in a situation with which it will cope — or not cope — in its own way. *Portrait in a Mirror* shows us a young artist seeing the world as beauty and yearning to interpret the beauty of the world through his art, but being caught up in the web of a passion that grows more and more sensual and disrupts his life, though not perhaps his work. In *The Fountain* we have Lewis Alison in search of, and seeming partly to have achieved, a central peace of spirit, but this too is disturbed by a love made up of sensual and intellectual elements: the main situation would thus appear to be not unlike the former one, but the handling and development are so utterly different that only analysis brings to light any similarity at all. Once again, *Sparkenbroke* presents us with a man whose soul's desire is illumination, an entry into spiritual reality that will come at death but may come earlier: he thinks he has found a means in love of a girl, but is prevented by pity from using her in the way he believes would be adequate to his purpose.

So far we have had three situations that are varieties of one situation, but since the three men faced with the situation are as different as three men could be who are all, in their way, artists, and since the situation is in each case worked out with completely different people and circumstances, the result is three novels not recognizably similar. Nevertheless Morgan doubtless felt that this situation had by now been sufficiently exploited, and for his next novel he puts a man who has no claim to be an artist into a totally new situation that presents him with a new problem: a man of simple nature and origin, framed by the gods to be divinely good, and, though loving a girl by no means obviously good, able to incorporate his love for her into his divine goodness, yet troubled and corrupted by the fact that he has inherited the charge of a prison and so is forced into a sin against liberty.

The Empty Room, short though it is, is more complicated, but the essential situation is that of a generous man confronted by the problem of an erring wife. *The Judge's Story* is the story of the spider and the fly—a good man in the toils of evil incarnate, seeing a simple if original path of escape while the poisonous creature drops off disappointed. *The River Line* shows us a man obsessed by a sense of guilt and finding deliverance in a strange and difficult love: the melodramatic happenings in France are, structurally, only there to account for his guilt complex. *A Breeze of Morning* seems to have a double theme, David's dream-like worship of Rose and the triangle of Rose, Howard and Ann, but the second is but an episode of the first, and its great value to the story is that it helps to differentiate it from that of Nigel's worship of Clare in *Portrait in a Mirror*. The last novel, *Challenge to Venus*, has two people in a not unfamiliar situation, one of violent sexual love. Their story forms a crossing pattern — they are apart, they come together, they are apart again.

It is plain that the novel in the hands of Charles Morgan is a single-focus novel, in accordance with the general practice of novelists of the last fifty years and in contrast to the multiple lines of interest bunched together in most Victorian novels. Sometimes we find two objects within the line of focus, but one is always comprehended under the other. In *The Fountain* the irruption of Narwitz into the picture undoubtedly brings a new and powerful interest, but he is essentially a factor in Alison's search for peace, shattering the concept he has so far formed and rebuilding it on stronger lines. In *Sparkenbroke* George Hardy's story has a serene life of its own, yet George is part of Mary's story as she is part of Sparkenbroke's. *The Judge's Story* is also the story of Vivien, but she is there to support and be supported by the Judge, and her resistance to Severidge's temptations is there to emphasize his weakness in yielding. I have pointed out the apparent duality but real singleness of theme both in *A Breeze of Morning* and in *The River Line*.

Other than the principles of making the beginning of a novel contain within itself the seed of the growing tree, and of confining the action to the clear working out of the situation confronting one character and its associates, I do not think Morgan can be said to use a technique of novel-writing, or generally accused of arranging his material in a pattern. The development of the action is completely organic, and it does not seem that the limiting of the action to the exploring of a single situation necessitates (as they said of Henry James) the crowding out of most of life. It is difficult to see that more 'life' could be packed into books like *The Fountain* and *The Voyage*, but the luxuriant material is not allowed to get out of hand: this is as noticeable in these long books as in the shorter ones that followed. I cannot do better than show this by outlining the action of one of the long novels and one of the short ones.

SPARKENBROKE

In a kind of prologue, Piers Tenniel, a boy of twelve, son of Lord Sparkenbroke, is shut by his brother into the Mound, the family burial place, and left there for some hours. He is not frightened, but undergoes a spiritual experience that for the rest of his life turns his mind towards death and its significance.

The story proper opens twenty-one years later. Piers is now Lord Sparkenbroke, and lives with his wife Etty and small son Richard at Sparkenbroke House near Chelmouth, a seaside town in Dorset. He is a poet and has a reputation as a seducer of women. His intimate boyhood friend, Dr George Hardy, a few years his senior, lives close by with his father, the Rector, and his sister Helen. A girl, Mary Leward, with her father and her fiancé, Peter, comes to stay at a Chelmouth hotel, and as she was once a pupil of Helen's she is invited to the Rectory. George falls in love with her (she is eighteen and very beautiful) and she likes him, but soon afterwards she meets Sparkenbroke by accident in a bookshop. She does not know who he is, but is dazzled by his brilliance and charm. Later she finds him, again by accident, reading near his cottage in Derry's Wood, and the conversation that ensues puts her completely under the spell of his personality. Sparkenbroke for his part has lustful thoughts about her, but afterwards finds that she has given him inspiration for his work. Mary meets him again by the bandstand in Chelmouth at night, and, discovering that he is the formidable Lord Sparkenbroke, is still further intrigued and charmed by his dominating quality and attentions to herself. She breaks off her engagement to Peter, and confides to George that her father has behaved so badly over this that she feels she cannot live with him, so George, now deeply but silently in love, suggests she should come and stay at the Rectory. She goes about with George on his visits, but sees Sparkenbroke often at the cottage, and ultimately it is tacitly understood between Piers and Mary that she will yield to his desire to lie with her. These meetings are known to no one, but at a garden-party George sees Piers and Mary together and realizes what there is between them. She tells George just what has been going on, and promises not to go to the cottage again, but she goes (being quite helpless in the matter) and is on the point of being seduced when either Sparkenbroke relents or she refuses — it is not clear which. George goes to the cottage and accuses Sparkenbroke of tampering with Mary, and Sparkenbroke leaves for Italy. Mary goes back to her own home, but presently, when her father dies, George persuades her to come back to the Rectory, where in due course he proposes and they marry.

Taking Helen (who is an invalid) with them they go for a holiday to Italy: George has to return to England, and Mary and Helen are left in Pisa. Helen is taken ill and in searching for a doctor Mary runs into Piers, who arranges for them to come and live in his Palazzo at Lucca. Sparkenbroke sees this as an opportunity to overcome Mary's resistance to copulation, but he is instead led to talk of his work, and again Mary inspires him to writing. After a time she conveys to Sparkenbroke that she will not permit him to be her lover, and he seems to accept this with relief. They continue to be desperately and quite beautifully in love, without any sign of obtrusive sex, till Helen dies and George comes out. The period that closes with George's arrival constitutes the climax of their relation — a beautiful and productive love – which could hardly have continued under changed circumstances.

Piers and Mary renounce each other, and she makes him swear never to tempt her to come to him. George and Mary leave for England, Sparkenbroke remaining in Italy to finish his poem on *Tristan and Iseult*. When this is finished he decides to return to England and start a new life with his wife. He goes home and begins to enter into his wife's social life, but he has a visionary experience that changes his mind, and he tells her he is going away with Mary. Mary is living happily with George, and tells him he need never be afraid she will cease to love him. Then Sparkenbroke comes and says she is to come away with him, and she agrees without hesitation. On the appointed evening she secretly leaves the house to join Sparkenbroke, but he does not turn up (really he is there watching her movements) so she tries to commit suicide and, failing, returns to the house, while Sparkenbroke goes to the Mound and dies from an attack of angina. George, who has been out on a case, finds Mary in bed, reads the note she had written and has forgotten to remove, realizes what has happened, but decides to keep his thoughts to himself, believing that this return is final.

THE JUDGE'S STORY

William Gaskony is a retired judge of sixty-six. He has a ward Vivien, whom he loves dearly because she is the daughter of Julia, whom he had loved in his youth but who had married his friend and is now dead. He has a much-prized copy of *Marius the Epicurean* that had been given to him by Julia. Vivien is married to Henry Lerrick, a young solicitor. George Severidge is the millionaire head of a huge industrial concern, and, though outwardly a kind and cultured person, is corrupted by the power his money gives him. His desire is to 'change' people, cause them to be untrue to themselves, and he is particularly anxious to get Gaskony into his power for this end. He has already, on a Mediterranean voyage in his yacht, wormed out of Gaskony the truth about Julia, and one day, at Rodd's club, of which they are both members, he induces the Judge to let him know how much he values his *Marius*. He offers to buy it for £250, but is of course rebuffed.

Henry Lerrick, though essentially honest, has been 'fiddling the cash' among the investments he holds in trust for his clients, and is in danger of being sent to prison for the embezzlement of £23,000. The Judge, being informed of the situation, says it is quite impossible for him to raise any such sum. At Rodd's Severidge baits Gaskony — in humorous, civilized terms — about his refusal to sell the *Marius*, and pushes up his offer to £2,500, which the Judge still ignores. Then Severidge enters his offer in the 'wager book' and — as if inadvertently — 'adds a nought', and on this being pointed out to him says he will stick to it. Realizing that this is the only way to save Henry and Vivien, Gaskony closes with the offer and promises to send the book. He goes home, posts the book, and on telling Severidge that he has done so is handed a cheque for £25,000, £23,000 of which is at once transferred to Henry's account. A week later Severidge denies having received the book (though we know he has done so), with the result that Gaskony feels compelled to return the money, most of which is no longer available. He consults his brother, who is the Head of an Oxford College, and they find that by realizing everything the Judge possesses, including his pension, they can pay back the £23,000 and just leave enough to bring in £150 a year. Without giving any explanation the Judge vanishes from London and takes very simple lodgings in Cliftonville with Lou Hagg, Vivien's one-time nurse. Here he is happier than ever before, for he is now able, without distraction, to get on with writing the book, *The Athenian*, for which he has been collecting material for years but has never till now been able to 'get down to'.

Vivien, who knows nothing of the financial transactions except that somehow, by 'Gasky's' help, Henry has been extracted from his perilous situation, thinks the Judge is away on holiday, but Severidge tells her he has discovered (through his spy system) that her guardian is living in unaccountably poor circumstances, and he and Vivien go down to Margate to investigate. Severidge goes first, and alone, to call on Gaskony, and learning something of the truth offers to make the Judge a present of the £25,000 so that he can come back to normal London life. But Gaskony refuses the offer, saying he has chosen this way of life for the sake of his writing, and that he is perfectly happy. Severidge departs in anger (for this is the first time Gaskony has flouted one of his temptations) and soon afterwards Vivien comes. She accepts and understands the Judge's new circumstances, but is in need of having her own problems set right. She is in danger of being deceived by Severidge's blandishments, of allowing her whole mind to be swayed and controlled by his corrupt ideals, and as a consequence she is drifting away from Henry. The Judge shows her how to look squarely at herself, to realize 'who she is', so that she is able to put Severidge's attraction behind her and turn again to her love for her husband.

These summaries should serve to show the action developing naturally and easily, but they give no more than the bare bones of the stories. The spirit that informs the body of the *Sparkenbroke* novel, the passionate search for mystical illumination that lies behind Sparkenbroke's love for Mary and distinguishes him from common seducers — this must be taken for granted in a summary; no summary of *The Judge's Story* could make clear the deadly struggle between evil and good, and the complicated series of temptations to which the representatives of good are subjected.

The two summaries have occupied much the same space, but far more even of action has had to be pruned out from *Sparkenbroke*. It is well known that after three very long novels, 'bursting at the seams' with psychological and philosophical implications, Morgan turned his hand to a new species, a novel with a classical spareness of bulk that perhaps gave greater satisfaction, though I myself would not lose a word — or more than a few words — from *The Fountain*, *Sparkenbroke* or *The Voyage*. (The first of the canon, *Portrait in a Mirror*, and the last, *Challenge to Venus*, are intermediate in length.)

A word about endings. Most of the novels give as much satisfaction in their end as in their beginning. *The Fountain* is, I think, an exception. The tangle into which Alison and Julie had got their lives was not to be straightened out by anything less drastic than a clean Gordian cut. Julie knew this, but Alison was less sure, so they set out, a little drearily, for home, and we are left wondering to what end. The problem of *The Empty Room*, again, seemed not to be soluble even by love and faith, so the last words of the novel leave us uncertain whether the prodigal wife is sweetly asleep or even more sweetly dead. (I believe the second was the author's intention.) The conclusion of *Challenge to Venus* repeats the conclusion of *A Breeze of Morning*: this is inartistic, except that a good thing should be capable of at least one repetition.

More interesting is the repetition, in *A Breeze of Morning*, of the situation that makes the plot of *Portrait in a Mirror*, the youthful passion of Nigel Frew, who is eighteen, for Clare Sibright, who is twenty-three. This developed on painfully sensual lines, so Morgan apparently decided to do it again, making the young man still younger, a boy of fourteen to fifteen, while leaving the difference in years between him and the girl much the same. The result is an entirely different and happier story, much more delightful to my way of thinking, and with a comedy (though in no way comic) ending in place of the hopeless petering out of the *Portrait*, with passion spent and remorse bitter — a fitting end to a tale of wilful folly.

The endings of the other novels evoke little but praise. The stark and pitiful events that occupy the four concluding chapters of *Sparkenbroke* are drawn at last into the wise and generous hands of George Hardy:

> A corner of the letter she had written stood out from beneath the candle-bowl. He drew it down and read it, and saw the great curve of the bowl-shadow leap up bed and wall. She has come back, she is safe, she has forgotten her letter; in the morning she herself must find it, believing it has not been read. Without ceasing to watch her eyes, he slid the letter into its envelope and, having closed it, reached out through the open doorway and returned it to its place.
>
> In silence he prepared for bed, withdrawing the light from her. Might he not go now and take her in his arms and comfort her, breaking her frozen secret? But he would not allow himself, at her cost, the passion of forgiveness. She has come back; she has chosen: she is safe, he repeated again and again; at last the thing has worked itself out; and it seemed to him that their life together depended upon his power to accept these facts and to let the night pass and the day come.
>
> At last, in this acceptance, going to his own bed, he lifted the candle that he might see her again. Her head had fallen over on the pillow; she sighed; perhaps, even, she was asleep. She has come back, he thought, she has chosen, and, wondering what her suffering had been, he saw on her flesh the dark stain of the rope. Then he might have cried out and awakened her; but he did not, for George was a man who always knew when to hold his tongue.

This is deliberately gracious and tender, and I accept it as such. Why not? Even more beautiful and appropriate are the concluding words of *The Voyage*:

> 'Well,' said Thérèse, 'here is our life beginning; together or apart — *our* life. What shall we do with it? Shall we make a plan?'

'Not now,' Barbet answered. 'When we are ready we shall know what to do.'

as it were, 'They, hand in hand, with wandering steps and slow [but Barbet and Thérèse were drifting lazily down the Seine], Through Eden took their solitary way.'

Supremely good, too, is the end of *The Judge's Story*. Gaskony has found peace, and has been able to comfort and strengthen Vivien in her resolve to resist Severidge and be at one with Henry. She asks him to quote a well-loved passage from *The Odyssey*, and when he has done so,

> She stooped and kissed him and went out. In the street, she raised her face to the wind, and Severidge saw her face, and fell back and let her go.
>
> The Judge climbed out of his bed and set his table in readiness for the morning. When all was done, he turned out his lamp and lay down, thinking of Nausicaa. 'This was the last word of the tale, when sweet sleep came speedily upon him ... unknitting the cares of his soul.'

Is this too deliberately beautiful? Let us leave that point for a moment. I do not find the ending of *The River Line* so satisfying, whether of the novel or the play, and I rather wonder that Morgan did not feel this, and work at both endings to make them more adequate to the fine story that leads up to them. The situation that had to be rounded off was certainly a difficult one, but Sturgess and Valerie loved each other, it was obvious that what he and the others had done was necessary (even if morally wrong), and the Victorian convention of vengeance required for a brother's blood (at least in fiction) was no longer operative, so something less contorted, less dubious and argumentative, would have pleased more.

A Breeze of Morning has two, if not three, endings. The story ends in a way when Rose decides not to go off with Howard, but David's part, the more interesting, ends with a picture of him thinking gloriously of the achieved scholarship — to the momentary forgetting of Rose, feeling that even she belonged to the past, while it is his future that is all important:

> My future was opening before me. It seemed odd that it should exist so brilliantly in me alone while my father and Ann and Howard and Rose were unaware of it. I stood in the road listening for the sound of carriage-wheels.

Then, after this conclusion, comes the tranquil, contenting matter of the epilogue, Rose married (and now dead), Ann happy with Howard, David writing the story of it all, the clock striking half-past ten, a star-lit night and all well.

The astonishing thing (already mentioned) about the ending of *Challenge to Venus* is that it so closely duplicates that of *A Breeze of Morning*, where Howard and Rose, lost in passion, arrange to go off together but at the last moment Rose sends David to tell Howard she is not coming. Now it is Martin and Fiammetta who, similarly lost, arrange to run away, but at the last moment Fiammetta sends Benedetto, the (rather older) David of this story, to tell Martin she is not coming, Fiammetta being left to marry Rinaldo as Rose had married Dick Featherford. The repeat was worth doing to show an English episode translated, as it were, into Italian, the reticence and mild annoyance that characterize the English change of plan in strong contrast to the excitement and emotion poured out by Fiammetta and Benedetto. Both endings are admirably effective, and if the last words of Benedetto which actually end the book are flat and hopeless, that is appropriate to a tale of futile passion.

It may help to explain some part of the critical disapprobation of Morgan to note that of the nine novels and two plays (the *River Line* play being ignored) only one, *Portrait in a Mirror*, has an ending that can be called tragic. We have noted some dubiety about the conclusion of *The Fountain*, and some ambiguity about that of *The Empty Room*. All the others leave at least a possibility open — even a probability — that the next stage will move into 'calme after stormie seas': as does sometimes happen in 'real life'. And this is not done by 'the waving of a magic wand': every ending, however happy, grows out of the preceding action, naturally if not always with necessity.

Let us look more closely at the charge that even all this rich and abundant action fails to account for important aspects of life, that most of life is crowded out to permit the construction of the Morgan scene. *Are* there 'no stupid, no poor, no bad'? In the section called *The World of the Novels* I have admitted that the proportion of 'bad' people is small, perhaps ten per cent of the number of 'good' characters. Can the reader of these novels declare that the proportion of 'bad' people among his own acquaintance is much larger than this? I have expressed a personal preference for the society — whether in life or in literature — of 'good' people, decent and kind people, and I can be much more emphatic about my dislike of stupid people. Here I have agreed that Morgan's picture is considerably out of true. I suppose we may class as stupid Ned Fullaton and Peter Darkin (to have a mind filled with cricket is almost a synonym for stupidity with Morgan), the Baron's family and perhaps Alison's mother, Mary's father, most of the Vincent family, schoolmaster Libbett again, and Dick Featherford (though 'Matho's' thickheadedness is combined with so much humility and good-nature that he is entirely delightful).*

Since stupidity is the commonest of human weaknesses it is obvious that there has here been some sacrifice of truth for the purpose of achieving what seems to me a very positive gain, the assurance of the constant company of intelligent people. As for 'no poor', this again cannot be denied, but I suppose Morgan recognized that he had not the gift of Dickens, Wells and Hardy of presenting the virtues and vices of the unprivileged classes. I do not think Morgan's refusal to deal with 'the poor' can be attributed to snobbery, since in those characters who came nearest to being poor — 'workers' such as the gardener in *The Fountain*, Sparkenbroke's man Bissett, sundry boatmen in *The Voyage*, Lou Hagg in *The Judge's Story*, the railway porter in *A Breeze*

---

* I am inclined to add the name of Commander Ferrers, on the same reasoning by which one might call Othello the biggest of Shakespeare's fools.

of Morning, and Guiseppe in *Challenge to Venus* — we have a handful of folk as delightful in their way as some at least of their 'betters'. The deficiency, if it is one, will matter less and less as poverty disappears.

It is all part of a question that was raised when I suggested — what indeed some readers impatiently assert — that some of the endings of the novels are too conscious of their own beauty: and the impatient asserters would not confine this criticism to the endings. But you have got to make your choice: either you like the romantic novel or you don't. Morgan is a romantic writer, and realism, if that term means a literal presentation of the ill-assorted superficial minutiae of everyday life, is not his aim. One can go farther and say that with Morgan the novel is a division of poetry, as it is with Hardy, Meredith, Stevenson and Conrad. I am not assenting to the heresy that 'poetry' can be written in 'prose', but allowing that it is possible to approach the novelist's material in the spirit of a poet. Morgan looks at the world through the high-powered lens of imagination, which brings order into chaos and permits the underlying pattern of beauty to be seen. The air of unreality that some readers think they perceive lying over his scenes is the effect of the arrangement of things and words to bring a deeper reality to light. There is rhythm in the lives of his characters as there is in the words they speak and the words used to describe them. Mary sways between restless passion and tranquil love till she comes to rest in George; Sparkenbroke between love and poetry till the hand of death steadies the pendulum. David swings deliciously between the beauty of Rose and the beauty of Virgil, Thérèse between the heady triumphs of Paris and the still delight of her 'voyages' with Barbet. More than once Morgan insists on wonder as the highest of human faculties, the attribute that places man nearest to God, and over all his world there is spread a transparency of wonder that shows life as infinitely more than getting and spending, something nearer to ultimate reality than the casual eye or commonplace fiction can comprehend. Everything has a deeper and lovelier meaning than it would have in prose existence.

Not only are the novels conceived with poetic intensity, they are conceived whole, constructed in the mind before being written. There are novelists who declare, almost brag, that their characters 'come alive' and 'run away with them', that they never know what they are going to do from one chapter to the next. This is a legitimate method, and I am sure it gives a special interest to the writing and (perhaps) to the reading of a novel. But I do not think it has been the method of the great novelists, or could result in a novel that is likely to endure. It is quite evidently not the method used by Morgan. Every one of his novels (and of course the plays — a play could not possibly be constructed on the don't-know-what's-coming plan) was plainly designed in all its major developments before pen was put to paper. Whether we have free-will or not we do not know, and, if we have, whether our free-will consists in choosing to do what our Creator has conceived us as doing, but that is the only kind of free-will known to the characters of novelists like George Eliot, Thomas Hardy and Charles Morgan.

Within the large poetic conception of a complete action there are passages written with great realistic power. The chapter with which *Portrait in a Mirror* opens gives a plain, exact and humorous picture of a family interior of the 1870s, and later there is an almost photographic account of a cricket match, with a brilliant catch by the dandiacal but competent Pug Trobey. In *The Fountain* the whole of the life in the Fort is done with a fidelity to fact due to a personally observing eye. *Sparkenbroke* and *The Voyage* are written with such continuous imaginative intensity that only certain pieces of dialogue can be thought of as lying within the realm of the humanly possible. There are some vividly true pictures of experience on the home front in the Second World War in *The Empty Room*, together with an all too realistic description of an alcoholic 'giving up' drink. In *The Judge's Story* the little episode of Henry negotiating with the Scottish lady about the sale of her Cennini is perhaps too exquisitely organized to be altogether of this world, but there is not a word that could not have been spoken by these two people. And take that scene in which Vivien, restless in the clutch of Severidge, shows how instinctively she is 'allergic' to him.

That night, when she and Henry were in their flat, she pulled out a book, opened it, shut it again and said:

'Why didn't Severidge fight in the last war?'

'I don't know. Why?'

'I thought everybody volunteered.' She rose from the chair-arm. 'I'm going to have a bath.'

'At two in the morning?'

'I am going to have a bath,' she insisted, emphatically separating the words. 'Put on a dressing-gown and come and talk to me.'

He carried in an ash-tray and sat beside the bath, smoking a cigarette.

'Do you suppose,' she asked, 'that Gasky's going to *live* in that place of Lou's?'

'Have you heard from him again?'

'Only once since he came up after Christmas. He says he's working. But he can't *live* in Margate, surely?'

'Do you miss him, Vivien? Is that the trouble?'

She lifted her face out of the sponge. 'Miss him? No. We have never clung.'

'Do you want to go down and see him?'

'When he wants me.'

'I thought,' said Henry, 'that might be — partly — why you are on edge.'

She turned on to her face and was silent while she rippled the water over her shoulders. 'You know,' she said, 'we're not his kind of people.'

'Whose kind? Gasky's?'

'Oh God,' she said, 'we're his kind all right! I'd come out of Margate long ago.'

Henry's smile was that with which he always confessed himself a laggard when she went too fast for him.

'I mean,' she said, 'in the next war you will fight ... Give me my towel.' ...

The whole of the granary episode in *The River Line* is done with great objective fidelity, while in *Challenge to Venus* much painful realism is put into depicting Fiammetta's lustful longing for Martin. But there is a kind of realism that goes beyond this, and is a special gift with Morgan — places where he is imagining things so intensely that one feels he is *there*, physically seeing and hearing, smelling and feeling. There is a Rembrantesque interior of the library at the Manor with Mr Letterby lighting the lamp: the huge untidy book-lined room is brought before us, with David in the arm-chair 'watching the match-light on my host's left ear and the window-light on his stooping back, in which the vertebrae appeared'. Another library scene with a three-dimensional quality is that of the Tower in *The Fountain* being shown to Alison by van Leyden:

> The books and shelves bore no accumulation of dust; the thick carpet gave out its faded colours; a broad central table, a reading-stand and a couple of shelf-ladders had been recently polished; a group of padlocked boxes, of the kind seen in lawyers' rooms, gleamed still, though their black enamel had been dimmed by the years; but there was no sign of common usage. On the table stood a dried inkpot, an empty pen-tray, a pink blotting-pad whitened by age, a wooden bowl of rusted pins.

The impression that Morgan is standing in the room is given edge by the dull gleam on the boxes and the whitened pink blotting-paper, and further still when the Baron presses the bell of a bicycle standing in a side room, and 'there was a grinding sound, weak and toneless, as if a mile away some little rusty gate had moved on its hinges'.

The mystic light that plays over *Sparkenbroke* does not preclude these personally felt moments. There is a shadow Mary sees as she sits in the cottage with Piers: 'yet she was reading a book; the page she was about to turn lay across her finger, the weight of the volume pressed her lap, and she knew that if she lowered her eyes from the gigantic head and shoulders cast in shadow on the opposite wall ... ' Another is of George outside the cottage in the rain: 'From the window of Piers's writing-room a patch of whiteness fell across the path and for a few brilliant inches climbed the opposite foliage. From this illumination the rain seemed to spring upward into the darkness.' A pleasant instance is that of the dog in the road (dogs are apt to turn up at critical moments in Morgan: there is a good one in *Challenge to Venus*): a situation of stress has arisen between Mary and Piers — 'she looked at the edge of the table and the scratches on its paint, and the still, matted head of a dog that stared up from the road, recording them' — and later, 'The sun had moved away from their table; a low wind was turning the chestnut leaves; the dog stood in the road and stared.' Morgan is not only there with them but remembers the occasion, for much later in the book Sparkenbroke, talking to a companion, thinks, 'only the future can be lost ... and he knew that he had lost the future then, at the small sunlit table, while the dog sat in the road and stared at them'. A grass-snake similarly remembered you can find for yourselves in *The Voyage*, but I cannot refrain from quoting the Roman snail from *The River Line*. One evening Sturgess sees 'a large Roman snail' patiently making its way over the lawn and wants to pick it up and put it on its way, but Julian says don't hurry the independent beast, and there is a small argument about it. Long afterwards we find Sturgess thinking of something Julian had done 'on the evening of the Roman snail'.

Between the brilliantly conceived incident and the organic progress of a complete action there is the scene, and here Morgan shows complete mastery over and over again. I can mention only a few. I suppose everyone recognizes the supreme effectiveness (both in novel and play) of the scene in the River Line granary that ends with the killing of 'Heron', with its strong elements of suspense and surprise, and the intriguing suspicion — that remains in the mind — that 'Heron', genuine British officer as he turned out to be, was not entirely free from guilt, or at least folly: undoubtedly he should have told his superior officer, Julian, what he had arranged to do in the way of writing to

Germany, and he clearly lied to Sturgess about the letter he had in his pocket. In lighter wise, yet most completely realized and made all-absorbing, there is the scene of the first meeting of David and Rose — how he comes into the hall, finds Rose and her companions vainly trying to rescue the squirrel from the chandelier, uses his quick intelligence to effect the rescue, and succumbs for ever to the magic of Rose's beauty.

> A girl was leaning out from the gallery ... I saw only the perilous leaning, the brilliance of the candlelit throat, her face eager and flushed, her wide eyes ablaze ... I continued to look up at the gallery as, at sea, I have watched a new moon ride out from a cloud. She was standing at the rail; the squirrel was in her arms; I saw her only and the squirrel's tail curling up into her hair ... she looked back at me with a kind of wonder at finding herself so regarded ... unaccustomed to the casting of spells so deep ... [and later] ... I turned and looked at her through my absurd, irrepressible tears. She was blurred and blazing ... I ran and ran.

Profounder is the first meeting of Lewis Alison and Narwitz. Alison has every reason to hate the thought of Julie's Prussian husband, and as he walks towards the castle hatred works in his mind like poison, calling up a succession of brutal and sensual images. Then he comes on the man himself, on the edge of a grassy bank — 'You must be Mr Alison. I have long hoped to see you. — Yes, I am Alison. — I am Narwitz.' After this Morgan puts all his strength into the task of making it come about naturally that the supreme beauty and humility of the mind of the German shall counteract the hostility of the Englishman and win him over to gaiety and quietness of soul, till Alison feels that he has the same pleasure in argument with Narwitz as an artist has in a drawing which flows with a rhythm of inward power, and he says within himself, Here is a great man, here is my master — to betray him is to betray myself: voicing the tragedy of the novel.

There are two other scenes of terrific power in *The Fountain*, one between Narwitz and Julie after he has been brought back dying from his hours in the storm on the island, the other the death of Narwitz. If the first is the greater it is because it is simpler and less conscious. But I do not know any living novelist who could have achieved any of these three.

There are many great scenes in *Sparkenbroke*. A very delightful one is that in which Mary, having turned Peter down and been stormed at by her father, goes walking, head down, in the rain, and is fetched in by George. It is one of those scenes that can be called 'inevitable': thought, feeling, talk all proceed on the lines they must inevitably have taken, without a word wrong. George comforts her with tea over the fire and orders her to relax.

> Her eyes opened and she smiled for the first time. 'I like being ordered.'
> 'Of course you do ... That's being free' —

He has in mind the good definition of liberty as willing obedience to law. As she sits there, breathing rhythmically, George is filled with 'that emotion towards beauty which ... is called love', and both are at peace. She tells him why and how she has broken with Peter, and how her father has behaved so badly that she feels she cannot go on living with him — she is afraid, not of her father, but of how lonely life will be, not 'peaceful and safe and lasting and good' like the Rectory where George lives with his father and Helen. So he persuades her to come and live there too for a time. 'I've been such a fool, George. I won't be ... Suppose you hadn't seen me and I'd gone by.' But that is not the way things happen in Morgan, or in life at its best. In strong contrast with this (and there is much similar contrast in *Sparkenbroke*) is the intensely written scene between Mary and Sparkenbroke at the bandstand, preluded by the charming incident of the cab-horse: the dialogue is lent ironic point by her ignorance of his identity. To her it is sheer fairy-land; he for his part cannot keep out lightning-flashes of poetry and philosophy.

Every reader of Morgan knows that every novel provides a number of these scenes, perfect in form and rich in content — the prison-riot in *The Voyage*, quelled by non-resistance and a box of glow-worms, going according to Barbet's imagination; the breathlessly exciting scene in *The Judge's Story* of temptation at the Margate hotel, with Vivien only just escaping;* and many more. There are a few that don't quite 'come off'. In *Sparkenbroke* the episode where Piers meets a young artist called Madden who has known Mary in her girlhood is not made credible; it reads like an interpolation to fill up the time Piers has to spend alone in Lucca. *The Empty Room* is the one novel written on a lower level, and more than one scene reads unsatisfactorily. The incident of Cannock listening to Rydal taking down a picture and carrying it upstairs, heaviness suggesting a body, is unconvincingly told; and other later scenes appear irritatingly melodramatic, hollow and false (perhaps only because I cannot like Venetia). The scene in *Challenge to Venus* when Martin and Fiammetta at last meet again after their night together is admirable in the first half, while Martin, with an amusing *naïveté*, is preparing her for his proposal of marriage, but ceases to ring true when Fiammetta begins to analyse, in long oracular speeches, herself and him and the situation existing between them: the Morgan method of getting into the minds of his characters seems to fail here. Some scenes between Thérèse and Courcelet are ruined in the same way by an unforgivable loquacity on the part of Thérèse (Morgan overestimates our interest in the minuter workings of her mind) — how different are the exquisitely natural passages, generally on or near the river, between Thérèse and Barbet. Once or twice in *The River Line* novel one feels uneasy at the length to which Sturgess's tale to Valerie and her godmother extends, but some of it is done in indirect narration so that one may suppose there was a summary without all the detail — which is indeed intended to supply the reader with a knowledge for which there was not to be room in the play.

It may be of interest to note that to match the great variety in the themes of the novels and plays there is considerable variety in the periods at which they are placed (there are no

* It recalls the more terrible scene — because the poor little victim did *not* escape — of Cleveland's seduction of July Conybeare in Rose Macaulay's *They were Defeated*.

'historical novels' except that in *The Voyage* the fictional happenings are closely paralleled by the domestic policies and personalities of Paris in the 'eighties). I will arrange them in chronological order:

Portrait in a Mirror..the 1870s
The Voyage 1883-86
A Breeze of Morning.circa 1900
The Fountain 1916-18
Sparkenbroke ....1925 — (prologue in 1904)
The Judge's Story......circa 1930
The Flashing Stream...1938
The Empty Room......1940
The River Line.........1947 with flash-back to 1943
Challenge to Venus ...1949
The Burning Glass ...'soon'

There is no attempt to show people as 'belonging to their period', except that in the *Portrait* the relation of parents to children is Victorian. Morgan's creations are not either temporary or contemporary — they rely on basic human nature and the common human situation.

The action of *The Voyage* is located in France; that of *Challenge to Venus* in Italy. In the two novels Morgan shows his great love and admiration for these two countries; for Italy also in parts of *Sparkenbroke*.

The three plays were all great stage successes, partly because of the sensational element in each of them. But they all play to a rising tension, with psychological truth in varied and fascinating characters. *The Flashing Stream* shows 'singleness of mind' carried to excess in a man of humourless intellect. It extracts vivid drama from a group of men working on a scientific invention in isolation, but finds it necessary to import two women, one good and one bad. Each (naturally) causes disturbance, and the two are at daggers drawn. The play is carried by the man who *has* a sense of humour, the First Lord, who, aided by the good, but not-too-good, woman, solves the psychological-scientific problem presented by the humourless Commander's stiff neck and ill-luck.

The River Line depends on the brilliantly successful second act, but this is fitted skilfully into the developing love of Sturgess and Valerie. This is a more human play than its predecessor, with a greater variety of character and action, and its basic idea, the necessity for maintaining a quiet spirit in an age of violence, more fruitful than singleness of mind, which needs careful watching if it is not to degenerate into monomania.

The Burning Glass is a play in which I can find no major defect. Its basic idea is both original and profound. The story, with its dramatic kidnapping of Terriford by the enemy, its scenes of painful suspense, its conflict on two levels, is all in one piece (not in two pieces, like *The River Line*). The characters are all deeply interesting: Christopher and Mary, with their love, their super-human memories, their chess-playing; an unusually 'sympathetic' mother; two shady characters in Tony Lack and Gerry Hardlipp; and a Prime Minister as good as Churchill himself, though in no way a portrait. The equilibrium attained at the end of this play is more complete than in either of the other two.

Whereas most of the novels are dominated by a love-situation, in the plays the love-interest is pale beside a more obviously 'dramatic' theme — the achievement of Scorpion, the killing of 'Heron', the use and mis-use of the Burning-glass. The success of the plays is a sidelight on Morgan's remarkable skill in the fashioning and control of a shapely 'action' in narrative.

CHAPTER TWO

People

WHAT ON earth can my friend have meant when he spoke of Fiammetta as 'the stock Morgan type'? The only characteristics she shares with other Morgan heroines are youth and beauty. It is true that a number of Morgan's leading women figures are young and beautiful: Clare, Julie, Mary, Rose, Carey, Fiammetta. But there are other young heroines who are not described as being specially beautiful: Ann, Thérèse, Vivien, though all of them produce an impression of having qualities hardly less attractive than beauty. At the same time it may be joyfully admitted that Morgan has a propensity to endow his heroines not only with beauty but with extreme beauty. I should find it hard to explain just why Rose Libbert seems to me to be queen of this garden of girls. Clare Sibright and Fiammetta have an equal degree of praise lavished upon them, yet it is Rose who dazzles me as she dazzled David, and I suppose it is because he is the youngest of the heroes, completely unspoilt by experience, so that the revealing lens of his personality is brighter and clearer than that of any other. Or is it just her name?

David's first glimpse of Rose comes through the ear — he hears a snatch of piano music, 'as though a kitten were playing lazily with a tinkling ball' — 'M' daughter', says the Squire. Next David hears from his father about her 'hair the colour of wheat', and though Mr Harbrook does not approve of her his voice softens as he speaks of her beauty, 'only skin-deep' — which is for David to judge for himself. Then comes the squirrel meeting, already described, when David's wondering and worshipping regard almost alarms Rose — 'You don't know what a frightfully ordinary person I am,' she warns him. As they all come out of church David is aware first of his sister's natural grace, 'of that

74

gentle and serene order which lights a face from within, as sunrise a quiet sky', and then (with a striking effect of contrast) of his 'visual sense' of Rose's extreme beauty: he looks, and looks away, 'driven away by that invading beauty as though it were indeed Aphrodite into whose face I looked'. Later when he joins in a ball-game he is fascinated by her poise and movement, as of a winged creature. He believes that he alone perceives the 'inward and unique endowment' of her beauty; he sees 'the head on the shield, but also the holder of the shield, of whom her visible beauty was mask and emblem'. Rose stands, in some sense, for Plato's 'absolute beauty'.

Dazzled as he is, David is aware that Rose is not an intellectual (though her quickness in realizing the significance of David's epitaph on her mother shows she is far from stupid) or indeed morally perfect. At one period he was discovering crack after crack in the exquisite fabric. He is sorry to hear that Rose has insisted that 'Matho' shall not be invited to the Seafords' dance; he feels a touch of worldliness in her voice, a likeness to her mother of ill-fame; he realizes that in teaching him French she 'can never tell me *why*'; he sees Rose and Howard at a dance, 'rubbing together intertwiningly, like cats'; he observes her bewilderment at a slanting joke of Howard's, and notes, 'there are minds that cannot jump a step'. But nothing lessens the 'dazzling blindness' of her beauty, and the relationship is a charming one. They discuss the possibility of her marrying Dick Featherford, and Rose, 'moving from seriousness to raillery', says,

> 'I believe I don't want to marry anyone ... except you! ... Then I shouldn't be bored and I shouldn't be frightened.'
> She came up from the piano and across the space that divided us in a single movement, and kissed me ... lightly, glancingly ... I put my arms round her, and kissed her — since her lips were there — on the lips. Inaccurately, alas ...
> 'Well,' she said, and no more then.

And we ought to take at its full value David's considered reply to Ann forty years later, when he had said he discovered a quality in Rose which she discovered in herself because he had discovered it in her, and Ann asked what this quality was.

> As soon as she asked it, I knew that there was no acceptable answer to that question ... The question was unanswerable, and my long silence became a burden.
> Then I saw a way in which a part of the answer might be given to Ann.
> 'She had the power,' I said, 'to work my "deep magics".'

This was a phrase they had used between them in their childhood, but one may suppose him to have meant now that Rose's beauty and personality spoke to the very depths of his spiritual self. It is to be noticed that though many years have passed both David and Howard are stirred by the news of her death — as they would hardly have been had she been just a pretty girl.

For Ann, David as her brother is incapable of a full appraisement of her looks, but we know she had a sweet human loveliness to match Rose's divine beauty, and she was certainly in herself worth two of Rose, who was yet 'the rose upon the rood of time', 'eternal beauty wandering on her way'.

It would be a pleasure to analyse the impression of great beauty set up by Morgan for Clare, Julie, Mary, Vivien, Carey and Fiammetta. Instead I will ask those who talk of a stock type to note how entirely different these girls are from one another. Clare Sibright falls in love with Nigel, five years her junior, but has no scruple in marrying Ned Fullaton, to whom she is sexually attracted, and then goes on to cultivate a sex-relation with Nigel, from the consummation of which neither gets anything but pain. Unlike Rose, Clare is something of an intellectual, and (according to Agatha Trobey) would like to have been the subject of a great spiritual painting but is not made that way. Julie, though still young, is a woman whose intellect can stand up to the companionship of both Alison and Narwitz; she is with some reluctance persuaded by Alison to enter upon sex-relations, but derives great delight from the relation while it lasts; afterwards she feels instinctively that her husband's death, with their betrayal of him, will always stand between herself and Alison. Vivien is the strongest of the younger heroines, and a very wonderful character. It is she who, right at the beginning, perceives Severidge's intention with regard to the Judge — to 'change him'. She is attracted by Severidge's flattering attentions, as Mary Leward is by those of Sparkenbroke, but retains an instinctive dislike for Severidge (who is a much more evil man than Sparkenbroke). She is the support of her husband, while she and Gaskony mutually support each other. Mary Leward, exquisite creature as she is, is on the contrary all too weak. This is not surprising, since she is the youngest of the heroines, only eighteen, and has for her tempter the celebrated Piers Sparkenbroke, a lord, notorious for his way with women, and able to play with Mary's emotions as a large and experienced cat does with a very small mouse. She 'loves' Sparkenbroke, but in his absence cheerfully marries George Hardy, and when Sparkenbroke beckons, goes to him hypnotically. Every movement of her vacillating mind is explicable and excusable, but the picture is none the less pitiful. Carey is a slight figure in a slight story, and leaves on the mind only a lovely impression of quietness. How other is it with Fiammetta! A terrific young woman, this: tall, beautiful, proud, a princess; daughter of a sex-sodden mother, yet trained by a saintly woman to live a life of austerity — till she meets the handsome Englishman and becomes drunk with desire, though retaining strength to refuse the suicidal course of marriage.

I suppose, of these seven, four share the common factor of experiencing strong sexual attraction towards a man, though I doubt whether Mary's feeling for Sparkenbroke had much to do with elemental sex; the other three are normal (or what seems to be normal in England, i.e. quiet, restrained, civilized) in their sex-relations. The little I have said about them shows them in other respects as different as primary colours, and the more you get to know about them in detail from their histories the more strongly individual they will be found. And what further variety is to be seen when those young female characters not distinguished by extreme beauty are lined up: Ann, Agatha, Ethel, Helen, Thérèse,

Madeleine, Karen, Valerie. And still there remain the women of a middle-age — sundry mothers, Lady Sparkenbroke and Lady Helston, Venetia and Marie, Mary Terriford ... And beyond these a wonderful group of old ladies: just think of old Miss Fullaton in the *Portrait*, of the two memorable French mothers, Mesdames Hazard and Vincent, of Mademoiselle Austerlitz at the reception desk of the Paris hotel ...

It is not to be supposed that Morgan was afraid or incapable of drawing a woman less perfect than these. There are Sophie van Leyden and some Vincent women. More interesting are the two women of *The Flashing Stream*, of whom Lady Helston, the Admiral's wife, is plainly intended to be 'horrid'. Her stage-description is — 'at once bright and intense — well-bred, well-dressed, affected, but no fool', but her behaviour betrays less equivocal qualities. One does not like her, but the action takes fire whenever she appears. Karen Selby, moreover, is not so 'good' that she cannot get a trifle mixed in her relations with the officers. Forcefully played by Miss Margaret Rawlings in the first production, she is the only intellectual woman in Morgan, and I don't know that I like her much better than Lady Helston. She spoils the second part — after the dinner-party — of the otherwise brilliant second scene of Act I. Her intervention between Ferrers and Lady Helston is a most unlikely piece of 'cheek' from a new-comer (who is also supposed to be 'well-bred'), and her long speech on mathematics as an art is quite inappropriate to the occasion. She goes on to declare that since she 'desires men' she will be a 'safe' member of an otherwise masculine mess; but such a woman (in spite of Morgan's defence in the Foreword), like the man-eating tiger, is apt to be undiscriminating in her choice of men to satisfy her 'desire'. It is worth observing that, unlike Karen's interference, noted above, Mary Terriford's stepping in between Christopher and the Prime Minister in *The Burning Glass* is as impeccable as it is effective, Mary being a woman of higher quality than Karen; her deliberate failure to stop Tony Lack's suicide showed her not only good but wise.

It seems undeniable that Morgan exhibits extraordinary power

in the faculty of creating a large number of women-characters
with literally nothing that can be called repetition except in the
matter of beauty, as to which, he who prefers the company of
plain women can be advised to go elsewhere. The range is even
more extensive when we come to look at the male characters.
Taking major characters only, there are some thirty of these,
young, not-so-young, and elderly. There are fewer young heroes
(and I shall take thirty as the first dividing line) than there were
young heroines — David (14-15), Nigel (18-19), Martin (25),
Henry and Howard (about 30). I have already said a good deal
about David, and Howard is a not very colourful person in the
same story, while Henry plays a minor part in the novel dominated
by his wife and her guardian, the Judge, with their enemy,
Severidge. Nigel Frew is the hero of the first novel, Martin Lyghe
of the last. It is a pity Nigel allowed his art to be disrupted by
love, because it is only as an artist and an art-critic that he is
remarkable. He has a vivid sense-imagination: thinking of the
possibility that he and Clare might have gone away together in a
carriage, 'I thrust my hand through the window of the carriage
and felt the air rush by'; imagining Clare asleep he sees her 'lying
on her left side, a bare forearm raised before her face. Soon she
will stir, I thought, and her eyes will open. Soon the fingers will
loosen and unfold'. But his imagination is not, like David's,
effective: it does not bring into being the thing imagined: he is
of commoner flesh; he is no worker of miracles. As an artist he is
solitary in a philistine world: he is pathetically excited when for
a moment a girl, his neighbour at a dinner-party, seems to have
entered into the spirit of his painting, but gets snubbed for his
mistake. As an artist he should have had the citadel of peace in
his heart, but only in his Parisian exile did he know 'the extraordinary seclusion, the sense of inward peace ... in a world quite
empty and silent'. The singleness of purpose that was his for a
year or two was split and torn by Clare, but Nigel was young
and doubtless re-achieved it in more permanent form — though
Jude Fawley, whose holy of holies was similarly, perhaps more
brutally, violated by Arabella, never did.

Martin Lyghe is about as different from Nigel as it is possible for two young men of the same nationality and the same class to be. He is tall, red-haired, self-confident, has been through Oxford and is otherwise experienced. Alone among Morgan's young men he is noticeably good looking, and as we know, good looks are one of the several untrustworthy criteria by which women are apt to be led into love.* When he is smitten by Fiammetta's beauty it is not as an artist; his poetic placing of her by way of Landor's *To Helen* is the only sign that he is inclined to cultural interests, except for a study of Italian that results in his speaking the language with an elegance and 'an ancient elaborateness' that delights Fiammetta's friends. In fact it is made clear that he is a sound young middle-class Englishman except for his moments of inspiration, of 'abrupt certainty', that generally lead to sudden effective action. He is less 'modern', more conventional, than most of Morgan's men, believing and feeling that love should definitely mean marriage. When Martin and Fiammetta — both of whom have up till now led lives of decent restraint — dine together for the first time and follow the dinner by going to bed as if it were the coffee course, we experience a noticeable sense of shock, which is greatly modified when we find next day that Martin regards this as a prelude to immediate marriage. His meticulous preparation of Fiammetta's mind to receive his proposal, by a detailed account (which an English girl would have found absorbing) of his family and prospects is amusing, and presently runs up against the rock of Fiammetta's indifference to anything but a continuation of sex-intercourse. The wise Sullivan sums it up neatly: 'The ironic gods put you two to bed together. And they did their piece. They worked their miracle. But they worked two distinct miracles.' But Martin cannot accept this and continues his efforts to persuade Fiammetta to come to Aden with him and enter into its 'small, bridge-playing colonialism'. Like Clym Yeobright in *The Return of the Native*, by sheer determination winning Eustacia over to becoming a schoolmaster's wife,

* And I wish some psychologist of aesthetics would explain why the lure of beauty when experienced by a man is a much safer guide.

Martin's 'fiery' character breaks down Fiammetta's instinct of repulsion, but in the end he yields to the inevitable and leaves for Aden alone.

Other than David Harbrook, who has a unique fascination for me, the most striking of Morgan's male creations are to be found in the middle-age group, between thirty and fifty. The ages are not always stated, but Lewis Alison, Piers Sparkenbroke, George Hardy, Barbet Hazard, Cannock, Sturgess, Julian Wyburton, 'Heron', and Christopher Terriford are obviously between thirty and forty, while Narwitz, Rydal, Severidge and Ferrers will be over forty. Here again, looking over the list of thirteen names, can one point to any sameness? Alison and Sparkenbroke are visionaries, but the first is prim and schoolmasterish beside the other, with his intense desire for mystic illumination and his Byronic attitude to women. George Hardy and Barbet Hazard are saints, but George is stolid English, Barbet's personality has wings. Three of the others share the homely attribute of loving their wives ...

I have already indicated my affection for Barbet Hazard, and as one reads one exclaims over and over again, 'How Morgan loves this chap!' — indeed he quite evidently loves Barbet and Thérèse as a couple. His detractors can make nothing of him. Lancret the priest, expressing resentment against Barbet's way of life, which completely ignores the Church, nevertheless admits, 'He is nearer God than I.' He bows to Thérèse's diagnosis, 'Barbet is a good man, innocent, almost sinless', and, seeking for a defect, can find only that he has 'excessive modesty'. Even this objection of the priest (whose mind is too badly inhibited for him to be a wise man) errs in the word 'excessive'. Like Gabriel Oak, Barbet is patient, and can wait without fretfulness for his desire to be fulfilled: he is unaggressive and has perfect humility; but he stands like a rock — a rock without hardness of outlines, mossy and flower-covered, but none the less a rock — against the blandishments, threats and pressures of the Vincent family, and he knows his own quality well enough. He walks with complete assurance into a jealous company of artists at the Ecurie Plence, and is at once accepted as 'the man who came out of the mirror'.

He has the wisdom of humility, and on his second visit to the Ecurie unassumingly silences the nonsense that is being talked. His whole virtue is of tranquillity: he possesses, effortlessly and surely, what Lewis Alison and Sparkenbroke were striving for and what Judge Gaskony achieved through disaster and poverty.

He is neither prig nor puritan, has 'lain with a woman' and can tell a lie to comfort Madame Vincent. He dislikes Thérèse's promiscuity, and even more her boasting about it, but sees through it to the essential decency of her soul, and by loving her and believing in her raises her at last to his own level. I have spoken of his imaginative faculty, by which he works his 'miracles', of his knowledge and love of birds, of his faith in the impulse that comes to him (and to others) from time to time that it is necessary to turn from the old ways and set out on 'a voyage'. He is always referred to as being 'little', and if some may consider him 'faultily faultless' he is not 'icily null', being endlessly interesting and a clear disproof of the fallacy that goodness is dull. Is he over-simplified? built round a formula? I don't think so. He is a different man in Paris from what he was in Roussignac. He is compact of love but is capable of hate. He is all-of-a-piece, but sane people generally are.

George Severidge is black against this shining white, a deliberate study of evil, and I suppose some readers find him more interesting. The devil incarnate, he holds the position which, next to a political dictatorship, affords more absolute power than any other in the modern world. The absolute power is exercised over the far-flung empire of his employees, and the wealth that goes with the position enables him to extend his power to others. Such great power has of course 'corrupted' him, but only because he was bad to start with: power does not necessarily 'corrupt' good people. He believes money will buy everything. There is an old lady in Glasgow who has refused him a rare manuscript, and he grins to himself as he thinks, 'She'd sell in the end. Everything was for sale. Meanwhile he was amused by her resistance, as he was by the resistance of younger women in other matters.' He has an itch to destroy good people, to change them, to prevent their being true to themselves. Above all he wants good people to admire him, to regard his power and personality as not those of a devil but of a god. In the New Testament story there is a wistful, hungry sound about the words of the Third Temptation: 'All these things will I give thee if thou wilt fall down and worship me', and this same sound echoes in a passage between Severidge and Vivien:

> 'Yes,' he said, 'you fear me, I know. But you needn't. I am not even going to say that I love you ... But what is true,' he went on, taking a match from a box and splitting it with his thumb-nail, 'what is true', he repeated, and let the box fall and scatter, 'is that I want more than anything on earth to be loved *by* you.'

(I suppose the business with the matches is to show his nervousness, due to the intensity of his hunger.) Again, when he visits Gaskony in his meagre rooms at Margate,

> He did not know why he had come — whether it was to peer at the downfall of a man he hated and regather him into his power, or to gain an admittance to an individuality he envied and would be loved by.

And speaking to Vivien about the visit he says, 'His is a friendship that I should enormously value ... it would change me. I want to be changed.' But Vivien is not deceived by the plaintive pseudo-confession — 'I wonder', she said doubtfully, 'or do you want to change others?' If we can forget that he is maleficent and a liar we may easily be dazzled by his lavish and kindly charm. He recalls the observation that E. M. Forster quotes from Melville, 'Natural depravity ... is without vices or small sins.'

It is this attribute that perhaps accounts for the last thing chronicled of him. Vivien has gone to visit Gaskony, Severidge has followed her and waits for her to come out of the house. Vivien has comforted and received comfort, and now, stooping to kiss her beloved Gasky, she goes out. 'In the street she raised her face to the wind, and Severidge saw her face, and fell back and let her go.' Or this may be the little inconsistency which is supposed to give solidity to a character in fiction. Or it may be just a matter of style — a dying fall to the sentence.

That question of inconsistency — I'm not quite clear on the necessity. Is it true that we all act out of character at some time or another? Certainly a well-drawn person should sometimes surprise the reader by some action, as Severidge does in his last abstention from evil. But when we have grasped the unexpected action we shall or ought to see that is not really out of line with the substance of the character. We are surprised when David begins to find flaws in the surface of his idol, but we soon see that this is a logical outcome of his intellectual quality. Barbet manages his affairs in Paris with more *savoir-faire* than we should have imagined a countryman could compass, but this is because we have ignorantly supposed that a saint must be a simpleton: it is indeed a beginning of our realization that Barbet has a very good head on him. When Rose at the last minute decides *not* to go off with Howard we may be as surprised as we are pleased, but we have only learnt something more about her — that like Sylvia she is kind as well as fair (or, if you are more cynically inclined, that she too has her head screwed on the right way). Without elaboration, I think the point may be taken that we have not finished with Morgan's characters till the end of the story has come. The last actions of Fiammetta, Venetia, Sparkenbroke, Tony Lack, all reflect back to throw a new light on the character as we have understood it up to that point.

But a clearer proof that Morgan's characters are alive is that they can at times let their minds wander irrelevantly, as George Hardy does when he sees a boy with a spade and a bucket, whereupon —

> he remembered that, in childhood, there is personality in a bucket; it is a proud, adventurous bucket with a legend and a future, just as a spade is a friendly, faithful spade, though a trifle dull because made of wood. An iron spade would be better. But it is dangerous, like all desirable things:

when you are older, an iron spade: when you are older, everything ...

A question in the same class is one I have heard raised by women — whether certain of Morgan's women and girls are credible in their relations with men, whether, for instance, Marie Chassaigne could have married Julian Wyburton, or Valerie Barton have accepted Philip Sturgess's love. The difficulties were mentioned in an earlier chapter. Of the three persons responsible for 'Heron's' death, Julian was the least guilty: Marie was more guilty, and may well have felt drawn towards Julian by the sharing of the guilt. She was rational, and French, and, as Sturgess noted, took, like Julian, a professional view of the deeds of war. None of these explanations applies to Valerie, but her nature was large and understanding, and she was deeply in love with Sturgess before the revelation gradually came to her.

Mary Leward's apparent possession of two lobes to her heart as well as to her brain, one for Piers and one for George, is more difficult to accept. (Would she be explained as a schizophrenic by the psychologists?) There is no doubt her mate was George, yet her love for him lacked an element of passion, in spite of which it probably endured and grew stronger with the years; her love for Piers, though seeming to be passionate, was really artificial and romantic. The facile passing from George to Piers and back looks fantastic, though men are supposed to find similar operations natural. She was a child between two men both 'old enough to have been her father', or nearly so, and clay in their hands. Let us hope she thanked God that death had left her for the one with the gentler touch, the one with whom she could know the sanity of happiness.

And Thérèse. Is it possible for a girl to love a good man and yet pass her life enjoying copulation with scores of casual comers, on occasion getting deeply involved in desire, as Thérèse did with Templéraud? It seems unlikely and it is certainly unpleasant, but I think Morgan convinces us that, given these two people, it is possible.

We have got away from our 'middle group' of men. In this middle group there are many worth studying, but an entirely unique character is Narwitz, Julie's Prussian husband in *The Fountain*. I have spoken of the impression of goodness he gives, partly through his capacity to endure suffering. In so far as this concerns the agony from his terrible war-wounds we may see in it simple heroism, helped by training and tradition. But Narwitz also underwent desperate spiritual pain from the realization that the love of Julie, his wife, whom he loved and trusted, had, in his absence on war-service, been transferred to Alison. He has known of the friendship before he arrived at the Castle from hospital, and no jealous thought has entered his head. When the Baroness urges that it will be impossible for him to meet Alison, Narwitz replies, 'But he is a student of Plato', and the two men quickly discover that they speak the same language. Then suddenly the truth about Julie comes to Narwitz; there have been signs, but he has ignored them, till suddenly they rush together as proof, and he is filled with — not anger but despair:

> He was a child whose mother's breast was entwined with adders; he was the dead summoned to resurrection whose saviour spat upon him and choked him with cerements. His head fell over on its cheek and a long shudder contorted his body. So he lay, smelling the hot odour of Sophie's flowers, and screaming in his throat soundlessly.

Yet afterwards he forces himself to continue the long philosophic conversations with Alison, and 'on the surface there was the same gentleness and patience', though the spiritual passion had gone out of him. Now and again we catch a glimpse of the Prussian officer as he exclaims against the military surrenders, but his steady purpose is to avoid earthly contacts and to teach himself to die. His last hours, culminating in his death, are entirely noble.

Lewis Alison, Julie's other lover, sometime tutor, is a figure of questionable merit, perhaps a man of pure intellect. He has broken off an understanding with a young woman of his own age and kind who evidently loved and was in tune with the academic side of his nature; almost compels his former pupil, now married, to become his mistress; and, though appalled by his realization of the depth of his betrayal of the husband, is not effectively moved by this and the consequent death. His greatest merit is that he is liked and admired by men, including the man he betrayed.

Just as we noticed with the women, some of the most fascinating and brilliantly drawn characters are to be found in the highest age-group. Beside old Trobey, the Baron van Leyden and Rector Hardy, the younger men in their respective novels seem to grow dim. Courcelet, with his intellectual and other distinction, may become boring on occasion, but he recognizes Barbet's quality as well as Thérèse's. Judge Gaskony, for all his weaknesses, has a secure place among those elderly men in fiction whom we most love and admire — old Jolyon Forsyte, Warden Harding, Bailie Nicol Jarvie. The astringent personality of Squire Letterby adds tang to the loveliness of *A Breeze of Morning*, as that of Count Ascanio does to the fervours of *Challenge to Venus*, where we also have the calm wisdom of the retired tutor, Sullivan. And in the plays the two political figures of the Prime Minister and the First Lord stand out with humorous strength.

For a purely secondary figure, Rector Hardy of *Sparkenbroke* is presented with what seems to me sheer perfection of drawing and endless interest in the portrait itself. When we meet him first in Book I he is not yet elderly, and all we learn of him is that he loves Tacitus, Swift and Goldsmith, and regards singleness of mind as the essence of art and of the teaching of Jesus. When we get to know him better old age is coming to him early, but his mind is composed, and beneath his critical intolerance there is an equable grace of spirit. 'His temper was quick, he was stubborn in his intellectual prides, he did not suffer the half-educated gladly, though he had a Christian hope of fools.' To him Piers Sparkenbroke's moral delinquency is unimportant as against his power to treat the great legends as if they belonged to a deathless spiritual world. George 'never knew what that old head was brewing', and was unable to adjust himself to his father's impish liveliness and incalculable simplicities. The Rector is more keenly aware than George is of Mary's confused state of mind at the time when she is engaged to Peter but has fallen under Sparkenbroke's spell. George says he doesn't see that it is any business of theirs, to which his father, with his inquiring intonation, 'No? Except that we are men and that she is beautiful and seems unhappy? Andromeda was not strictly the business of Perseus?' He has learnt much from experience: when George tells him, 'Your sudden challenges frighten people. They're not used to being taken at one bound into the heart of a subject', he answers, 'Better if they were. Half of life is wasted on neutral ground.' One of the best scenes in the novels is the one in which the Rector construes 'a bit of Catullus' that Sparkenbroke has been translating. The whole scene is sheer delight, and reaches its humorous climax when Mr Hardy asks George —

> 'And look at '*atque*' — why not *et*?'
> 'Because it wouldn't scan.'
> The Rector threw his napkin on the floor. 'Wouldn't scan! Wouldn't scan! There's the Lower Fourth kindly excusing Catullus! For heaven's sake let us assume that Catullus knew his trade! ... '

Then the Baron, Oom Pieter: it is against the abiding background of his unostentatious kindness and deep rectitude that the passions of *The Fountain* are played out. It is he who puts them once and for all in their place when he comes to Julie after Narwitz's death and secures from her an admission of what has been going on.

> 'But, Julie,' he said, 'I'm not a preacher — God knows. But here you were, sent here by your husband, under my roof, under my protection. And he was at the wars — not his own fault he left you. I was pledged for you. You were doubly pledged. You were my daughter — I've always seen you so.' ... After a long pause he added, 'You've let me down'.

Julie says, 'I'm sorry you should hate me.'

'Not hate you, child. God forbid.'

'Despise me, then. Feel that I ... '

He did not deny it ... 'Well, there's no more to be said, Julie.' And he went out.

There are crowds of minor figures, people who impinge upon a story at the relevant point and, having made their impression, vanish from the scene. Such is Mr Doggin, Nigel's first art-teacher: not only does he give voice to some of the principles of art of which the novel is full, but it is he who finally persuades Nigel to return to Windrush to finish the portrait of Clare, though he understands Nigel's reluctance: 'Then go,' he repeated. 'Fear nothing. Only the little men turn aside from walking with devils and angels. You will find God in no other company.' Another is the Italian doctor who attends Helen in Lucca and converses with Sparkenbroke, putting Piers's fantasies into commonplace form. And there is 'Matho' himself, Dick Featherford with his 'vintage' car, a more central figure but given the slightest of sketches: he loves Rose, is puzzled but unruffled by her ridicule, and tells David she is 'a good girl, really' — he may have made her a better husband than either Howard or David would. And Maria Guerini, Benedetto's mother in *Challenge to Venus*, who brings relief to Martin's afflicted mind with the gentle wisdom of her experience:

'I have flashes of vision, but I am not a visionary; I am an ordinary pious woman ... To accept one's limitations without disappointment — that is hardest of all ... Only among men is unlikeness called inequality, and sometimes thought of as an injustice ... There are such things as false certainties ... which have, I mean, the *feel* of faith itself but which do not lead to truth.'

(This last was a warning to Martin, and was a mistake Barbet never made.) There are more of these little portraits than can be counted, and each is done with a miniaturist's skill.

89

My admiration and liking for so many of the inhabitants of
Morgan's shadow-world has prompted me to weary the reader
with descriptions of them, but I cannot leave out a little group that
has an unending attraction for me — the two lovers, Madeleine
and Cugnot in *The Voyage*. They are figures of the background
of the novel, the two most colourful personages of the Parisian
world of artists into which Barbet finds himself pitched when he
goes in search of Thérèse, yet eye and heart dwell lovingly on the
gracious picture they provide. We meet them first at the Ecurie
Plence, and Madeleine at once establishes their relation. Cugnot,
a brilliant and fantastic figure, has been the first to accept the
inadvertent intruder as 'the man who came out of the mirror',
and now makes an extravagant speech, ending with, 'My vice is —
what is my vice, Madeleine?'

> 'Ah,' said the girl who held his glass — a girl with deep
> violet eyes, a full mouth, and the high, rounded cheeks of
> a child, 'your vice, Cugnot, is that you make speeches. You
> make a speech when I am taking off your shoes. My vice is
> that I take them off.'

Presently we are told that 'even when she was looking elsewhere
or talking to others she seemed to have Cugnot in her charge'.
It is she who explains to Thérèse that the basis of service is not
duty but love. There is the pathos of precariousness in the
relationship, but Cugnot is not unworthy — the picture would
otherwise have been ugly, like the contrasted picture of Thérèse
with Templéraud. Cugnot does not love Madeleine as she loves
him, but he is faithful to her, and gentle. He neglects her sometimes, but she has the gift of accepting his neglect as if she did not
mind it. The two are always there, a bright, mild spot of illumination among the dusky, dubious crowd of Thérèse's admirers,
and she would sometimes break away from the restless company
and visit them in their studio 'because it was unchanged, and
because nothing in their manner bowed down to her new fame'.
They have no effect on the action, but their presence sweetens
the sense of Thérèse's feverish life in Paris.

It is noteworthy that there are twice as many interesting fathers in Morgan as mothers. In fact most of the young heroines are totally deprived of maternal support. Clare is an orphan, Julie has but a brainless step-mother, Carey an absentee mother; we know that Rose and Fiammetta once had mothers from whom they inherited what bad qualities we may see in them; Thérèse is illegitimate and her mother is long since dead; Mary, Valerie and Vivien have no mother living. It is distinctly odd, and one can only suppose that Morgan preferred to see girls standing on their own feet like Sue Bridehead and Becky Sharp instead of being mother-ridden like Tess or mother-resistant like Beatrice.*

The facts are in strong contrast to the excellent father-relationships enjoyed by Nigel, George, Richard, David and Carey, while Vivien has almost more than a father in 'Gasky'. Lewis Alison's mother is inclined to nag, and the only exceptions to the general picture are to be seen in the profound and instinctive link between Barbet and his mother and the pleasant relationship between Christopher Terriford and his.

There are very few children, though those few are exquisitely presented. David Harbrook is a good deal more than a child, and Lou's son, the Judge's god-child, called William Vivien, who puts up an owl-knocker against 'Mr Gasky's' arrival, is thirteen, but young Richard Sparkenbroke is delightful at six, and less precocious than his father had been at twelve. He liked Dr George to tell him stories — 'about a Dolphin who had three sons'. George begins:

> 'Once upon a time there was a dolphin who lived in Italy, and he had one son.'
> 'Three,' said Richard.
> 'One,' said George, 'to start with.'

There is a 'pale-faced, yellow-haired little girl, idle, bored, dangling her feet', who sits with her nursemaid and watches Vivien in the shelter at Margate, and is reproved by the nursemaid for

* Morgan's mother died when he was a boy, but he need not have gone to this length in reaction.

commenting, 'Oh, what a big sigh!' This little girl is a dim recollection of that other charming and quite wonderful little girl who glimmers on the horizon of Thérèse's life at a happy moment while she is waiting for Barbet on the Pont d'Austerlitz. She insists that the Seine is the Mediterranean Sea and makes her great-grandfather tell Thérèse his personal story of the return of Napoleon. As they part, 'Please, who are you?' said the little girl. 'Thérèse Despreux.' 'Are you famous? May I touch you?' ... Thérèse, alone again, stretches out her hands to feel the sun, and is presently accosted by a young man who thinks he can 'get off' with her: she is kind but firm, and he goes into his place, but when he says she looks so 'content' and she asks him if he too is not happy —

> at once he fell in love with her and began to tell her the story of his life.
> 'Now, listen,' she said. 'I like you. Goodbye.'

These are things that do happen to one when one is happy and in the mood.

I have shown that Morgan's characters live, by whatever test may be applied. Do they grow? — and are they affected by their own actions, more especially do their moral lapses bring about moral deterioration? I must lead off this last question with a negative instance: I think the kind of life Thérèse lived in Paris — the promiscuity she so horribly detailed to Barbet, and in particular the disgusting submission of her central soul to Templéraud — must have shown its effect in a soilure of her personality, yet she grows more delightful as the tale proceeds. Morgan — and Barbet — would have said this proves her moral soundness: a really healthy person can walk through a fever hospital and emerge uninfected. The apology is only partially acceptable: it is Morgan himself who says that desire for Templéraud grew 'like fungus' on Thérèse's brain, and you do not get rid of fungus by walking away from it.

Otherwise I think Howard, Alison and Julie all show signs of degeneration in consequence of their follies and sins. Sparkenbroke's case is parallel with Thérèse's, not in moral soundness but in intellectual integrity. Sparkenbroke's whole life, in its 'right' and 'wrong' aspects, was so completely under the control of his mind and will and artistic purpose that the effect of delinquency would be minimized. But his sudden decision to take Mary from George in spite of his oath and the demands of decency and loyalty would indicate a frightful degeneration if it were not followed by his abandonment of his purpose when he saw she was accepting it against the instinct of her soul — and even this only excuses him on one score.

'Growth' requires time, and not all Morgan's novels cover a period long enough for growth to be noticeable. Nigel Frew changes in four or five years from an innocent boy to a broodingly introspective young man, and his view of art and beauty goes through several stages of development. The characters of Alison, George Hardy and Barbet are firm-set when their stories open, and all we can perceive is that Alison grows a little weaker, George and Barbet a little stronger — Barbet and Thérèse undoubtedly develop side by side. There are a few characters drawn deliberately static, like Courcelet and Victor Vincent.

Having in mind these scores of created characters, vivid, vital, every one different and every one crammed with colour and significance, I feel it is difficult to deny to Charles Morgan a gift of portraiture as authentic as that of any novelist of the century.

CHAPTER THREE

Style

(a) *Prose*

As WITH people, so with prose: there are two kinds, rich and poor, and one is as good as the other. Or sherry, dry and sweet: most 'educated palates' prefer dry, but sweet sherry has its hour. But in the matter of prose, the critic of today is given to asserting that for modern ears there is only one acceptable prose, the plain and informal, the style that is no style, which gets its meaning across, indeed, but does nothing else, gives no pleasure in the process. No art critic, of today or yesterday, ever made this claim — that that picture of Peele Castle is best which shows you the castle plainly, stone upon stone, without 'the gleam, the light that never was on sea or land'. Not that the 'dry' style in the classic writers was ever to be so described, or was as meagre as it has become today. George Saintsbury, the last great critic to value the sonorous prose of Shakespeare, Browne, Ruskin, Pater, was well aware of the other glory of the economic prose of Swift and Goldsmith. Morgan himself shows high appreciation of the second kind in the lesson that Rector Hardy gave to young Piers Sparkenbroke on the difference between the Seventeenth- and Eighteenth-Century writers, with Stendhal's rule of 'clearness' thrown in for good measure. But Morgan's masters are the writers of the harmonious imaginative prose of the Seventeenth Century, chiefly the translators of the Authorized Version, and his own style has the elaboration of a symphony. But the symphony is of Mozartian clarity: he wrote approvingly of Sparkenbroke's method: 'His composition was slow, for he cared above all else to give, even to complex thought, a verbal sequence of the utmost lucidity; thought might be dark, but, the more elaborate the music, the more precise must the playing be.'

In the following passage there is no darkness of thought, but the writing exemplifies the principles described:

> So day by day he withdrew within the circles of consciousness towards the centre of his being, little disturbed even by the knowledge that the solitude of his present life could not endure. Nights of dreamless sleep were followed by the vigour of the morning, given always to new work, for his history moved forward now, swift and smooth. In the afternoons he revised old pages, allowing an interval of several days to pass between writing and revision; and in the evenings, among his books or on foot across the moors, he allowed other men's genius or his own experience to flow in upon him, not compelling himself to learn from them purposefully or in a way prescribed, but happy that they should teach him as they would, like wise travellers encountered fortunately who walked with him a little while until their road parted from his.

> (*The Fountain*)

Observe the rhythmic arrangement of the three sentences, short, shorter and long. Within each a varied inner rhythm prevails, most noticeably in the third. Prose of this kind, where the rhythmic form, though eschewing the ultimate magic of metre, aims at a purpose of communication not unlike that of verse, should be read with at least a sense of the pauses that mark the rhythmic units.

The strong control that the method demands permits modifications to deal with moments of intense feeling without going over the edge of sentimentalism. The great scene of Narwitz's death ends with absolute force and economy:

> She would have kissed him, but when he felt her touch upon his shoulders he said, 'Leave me. I wish to forget even your kiss … I wish to be alone.'
>
> When they were far from him, he asked:
>
> 'Am I alone?' And after a long interval he said, 'My Julie … '

She did not stir, nor Lewis at her side.

And he cried aloud and said in his own language: 'Into thy hands I commend my spirit', and when he had spoken thus, he gave up the ghost.

This laconicism was not achieved without effort. We know that the last part of the passage was originally written:

She did not stir, nor Lewis at her side.

At last he smiled and said in German, as though he were repeating a fragment of a fairy-tale that comforted him, 'Into Thy hands I commend my spirit', and when he had spoken thus the spirit left him.

There is obvious gain in the omission of the too specific 'German'; the change from 'Thy' to 'thy' is consistent with Narwitz's known religious views (he may now have meant into Julie's hands); the long phrase about the fairy-tale would have held up the brief scene; perhaps the 'smiled' might have been retained to suggest the thought passing through his mind, but it would have detracted from the tragic tone. The final form has obvious echoes from the story of the crucifixion.

Evidence of the influence of the style of the Authorized Version is not often explicit, but the long concluding paragraph of Chapter V of *The Sparkenbroke Mound*, beginning, 'At the entrance to the Mound, when the gate was back and his way stood open, he hesitated, and Stephen, supposing that he was afraid, taunted him', bears the impress.

I have spoken of the strong control necessary to keep this kind of prose from running away into lushness. After the *Portrait* Morgan's hand on the reins never slackens, but in that first beautiful book the discipline has not yet been fully established. There is, for instance, a passage (in Part IV) where Nigel lies on the floor contemplating the riddle presented by the drawings he has made of Clare. He marvels at her beauty and at the love he feels in his heart. And he goes on marvelling for three and a half pages, his thoughts growing wilder and the language more and more extravagant till one longs for the missing sense of humour that would have dried up the flow at the source. How different, how completely satisfying, is the equally long passage in *Sparkenbroke* (Book II, Chapter XIV) where Piers, looking in at the window of his cottage, sees Mary sitting there. She has her back to him, and before making his presence known he lets his mind dwell not only on the artistic repose of her posture but on the two writings on which he is engaged, so that he had, 'in that instant, three lives — one of Tristan's ship, another of the miraculous voyage that brought the holy image to Italy, a third of his actual experience as he looked through the window of Derry's Cottage. They were not, in his consciousness, divided. To imagine was to live, to live was to imagine'. In all this long passage there is not an unnecessary word, a displaced rhythm, a thought that is not bound by logic and imagination to what is before and after it. The mind of the writer works with precision, the artist's hand is in control all the time.

Not that the passage described as undisciplined from *Portrait in a Mirror* is a fair example of the prose of that novel, which would be better represented by the paragraph describing Nigel's recovery from depression:

But one day of early spring, when the contrast between Nature's increasing life and the death within myself had become unendurable, I went out alone and climbed a hill. It was approached by a long grassy slope known to me since my childhood, and, as I mounted it, the quiet, steady effort calmed me. The living face of Nature, which hitherto had seemed to menace me, looked kindly into my isolated and frozen heart. More than ever was I solitary, but my solitude took on a glory which it had never before possessed. When I reached the summit, I lay down upon the springing turf and hid my face amid the grass and thyme. I felt earth's heat below and the heat of the sun above me. My eyes, pressed close to the brilliant forest of the grasses, seemed to penetrate the depths of the earth, and my outspread arms to

G

feel its mass clasped in their embrace. I became aware, with an extraordinary delight, of my physical smallness, but was not frightened, or forced into insignificance by this experience, as by the presence of great machinery or of human beings in mass. I was at once exalted and comforted. I felt myself absorbed in the open vastness of the universe about me. The agonies of particular memory and disappointment, the hurts to pride, all the wounds of human intercourse that had tormented me were reduced to the proportion of the body which lay as a speck upon the curve of earth; my spirit sprang up, marched with the giants, took wings among the gods. The courage to create awoke in me; joy, a tide from earth and heaven, found me and swept me forward; a sweetness, like the sweetness of early morning at sea, hung on the breeze that lifted my hair and flowed in upon my parted lips. I was identified with that day of sap and resurrection, and lay still with an emotion pouring from me which had in it the passion, but not the supplication, of prayer.

The content of this lovely piece recalls not only the passage in Book IV of *The Prelude* in which the young Wordsworth dedicates himself anew to poetry (Nigel says in the next paragraph, 'To this secret life I dedicated myself'), but even more closely the beginning of *The Story of my Heart* in which Jefferies, at just Nigel's age, climbs just such a hill and goes through much the same experience, though carrying it on to greater heights of mysticism. There is little to choose between the quality of one and the other for sheer prose excellence, though as Morgan's is more consciously beautiful perhaps the palm must be given to Jefferies.

It is only in this first novel that one catches an occasional echo of a blank verse rhythm:

> Clocks chimed through open sunlit doors; a dog
> Slept in a stream of gold;

or again,

                                 How
I should remember them when they were ended!
How in old age I do remember them!
Here were finality and content. No need
(To struggle or make plans. The day was not come; the
      world slept);
Gaze on, gaze on, hear her slow breath. Be still.

This is beautiful, but there is a rule that the most emotional
prose ought not to invoke the aid of metre to achieve beauty, and
I think Morgan avoided the practice altogether after the *Portrait*.

The prose of *The Voyage* is less formal than that of the preceding novels. The scene of Madame Hazard's death is as fine
in its simpler way as that of Narwitz:

> This vigil continued many hours. Others came and went,
> and Barbet was not disturbed by them. Twice he rose and
> touched his mother's face, then returned to his chair. In
> the late afternoon her eyelids closed and she said:
> 'The door was open, Barbet.'
> 'Yes, mother.'
> 'It was foolish of us not to know it until then.'
> For an hour she did not speak; then she began:
> 'I supposed once that you would raise me from the dead.
> It is not necessary.' After a little while she added: 'When you
> grow old, Thérèse, do not say goodbye to the nightingale.
> It is not necessary.' She sighed deeply. 'Nothing vanishes.'
> Then, in a stronger voice, her normal voice: 'Barbet, please
> take my face between your hands.' When he had done so and
> kissed her, she opened her eyes, and continued to live
> until the evening, saying no more and, it might have been
> supposed, sightless. But Barbet did not take his eyes from
> hers until she died.

We hear a good plain man thinking in good plain prose when
Thérèse asks Barbet whether he wouldn't like a few medals —

> 'What should I do with them?' he answered. 'To be a

vine-grower is a good life for me, though I'd rather be a cooper and not own the place. But as I'm not a shipper as well, I couldn't make a fortune if I wanted to. Most of what I do make goes back into the land; I like that. And the work gives me a chance to see great things in little: in the bud, the grape; in the grape, the wine. The wine has the earth and the sun in it. In one of Quessot's barrels there's the whole round of the year. And, behind the turn of the seasons, sometimes I can see a bit of the life of man, and behind that — it's hard to tell, but I do feel it, Thérèse ... '

And it is with a plain though beautifully managed prose that Morgan creates atmosphere, both of a scene and of a temperament, when, as an after-supper game of piquet proceeds, Thérèse again asks Barbet a question:

Barbet held his cards against him and listened, then continued his game. Thérèse knew that his imagination had carried him into the cells with his prisoners, and when their game was done, the players at the other end of the table still continuing, she was content to sit opposite him, wordless, and to watch his face. As long as he and she might sit thus and the priest and Madame Hazard mutter and exclaim over the slap and patter of their cards, so long would this stage of the evening last, and Thérèse found rest in it; she did not want time to move forward into questions and action; she wanted to be as she now was, near to him and silent, still living in the very evening in which he had first taken her in his arms, not looking back upon it as she would tomorrow look back out of her own separated experience, but lodged in his life, a part of his actual recognitions. Nevertheless she began soon to try to engrave upon her memory his face as she now saw it ...

There is in contrast a headiness about the prose of *Sparkenbroke* — nothing overdone, but in keeping with the high tension of the story. Mary, at the seaside, steps out of the hotel before going to bed:

> The night came upon her with the rush of surprise, like the scent of a garden that is entered from an airless house; not through gradual perception, adding beam to beam, shadow to shadow, but with single impact, fluid and alight. Music came to her, but not as a distinct recognition; it showered in the air, and the air had music's lilt, which, upon its lightness, bore a melancholy that was the sea; and, out of the following hush, when distant applause fluttered up and died like the turning of leaves in the wind, sprang the arched remoteness of the sky. Night was all hers; hers the stream of heaven; for her the little waves slapped and hissed on the beach and the bronze lion at the drinking fountain held silver in his teeth ... The breeze was under her hair and she alive. She tasted the faint salt on her lips and plunged into the stream of people ...

Yet we have to remember the quietness of the book's close, with George and the candle beside Mary's bed.

In *The Judge's Story* the style is both easy and exact. The opening paragraph rings with the tone appropriate to the man who is to dominate the story:

> At the Royal Automobile Club, to which he belonged for the sake of its swimming-bath and because it was near to Rodd's, Severidge had swum four lengths and eaten four sandwiches. This energetic and frugal process had been accurately timed. It was not his habit to be either early or late. No timepiece ever contradicted him unless it was wrong, and when he looked inquiringly at the post-office clock at the bottom of St James's, it replied obediently: 'Two-thirteen.' At a quarter past, he would be on the steps of Rodd's. In that ancient club, he would drink a glass of brown sherry and play one rubber of bridge. From three-fifteen his car would be waiting for him. At three-forty-five or

earlier he would be back in the chairman's room of Combined Metallurgical Industries — his first afternoon appointment, with Haslip of the Treasury, was at three-fifty — and would work there until he drove back to South Street to dress for dinner.

And much later, with a concentration of purpose springing from Morgan's detestation of the man:

... and he began to desire the girl, not frivolously and casually, nor with a lascivious hunger, but with the desire of the deaf for hearing as they watch the movement of a stream. He desired the marriage, which was the girl's integrity, rather than the girl herself. It presented itself to him as a great sheet of paper may present itself to a man who is not an artist — as a reproach and challenge to his incapacity, as something to be scrawled upon.

Note the immense force of the figures. Or take the lovely 'interior' which is the first chapter of Gaskony's new simple life with Vivien's old nurse. It finishes with this paragraph, and those who say Morgan's style is ponderous or over-elaborate should read it:

He enjoyed sitting with Lou by the kitchen range, and, as he told her his working routine, his spirits rose. She had an oil-lamp; she would trim it now, and he should take it upstairs when he went to bed. That there was a lamp after all gave him keen pleasure; it seemed to him an omen; as though it had been awaiting his need, it annulled his sense of being an outcast. While he watched the hands filling and lighting it, as though they were impersonal hands less real than the lamp itself, he looked up at Lou's straight dark brows and the little mole on her left cheek and thought gladly: While I am climbing the stairs, it is her life that will be continuing here; here, in Lou, will be the centre of all time and space, as it was in my Athenian, and in Nausicaa when Odysseus climbed on to her beach. He took the lamp, said goodnight, and started on his way. Now if only I could get that on to paper, he thought, then my book wouldn't be a period piece; it would be timeless — true from the inside outwards. Upstairs, in his striped pyjamas, he said his prayers for custom's sake. He said them standing, as he was about to get into bed: first, 'Lighten our darkness ... ', fast and silently, then his own aloud — six monosyllables used every night for over fifty years: 'God, make me fit to write.' Before he was fourteen, he had asked: 'O God, help me to write a great book', but in his fifteenth year had amended the plea. 'God, make me fit to write', he said, and slid between the sheets. God, who could read shorthand, would not object to this: it was not a demand-note; it was not a prayer for results. It was from the inside outward, as near as he could make it; and left to the Court a wide and, he hoped, a merciful discretion.

Now *The River Line* was, we are told, written in a mood of hesitation between novel and play, and this seems to me to have produced an effect of excessive deliberation in the prose of the novel. The landscape here is *too* carefully noted:

The sun, declining among patches of cumulus towards the high wood where Sturgess had spent the afternoon, thrust a long dagger of gold down the valley's eastward-looking slope and wiped his blade along its ridges. Over the opposite hill above Tarryford the web of twilight, woven first on the river's bank, was drawn slowly upward. A herd of cattle on low ground, which a moment earlier had glowed like brass on the intense green of that moulded earth, faded; the earth under them flattened; and inch by inch the roots, the trunks, the branches of the trees above were flooded by the mounting dusk. As yet the upper ranges of elm and oak held a liquid fire, and seemed, at their translucent edge, to diffuse it, as a nimbus, against the steadily reflecting sky. Soon they too would be gone but there was a moment when, it seemed, evening was poised between sunshine and dusk, and birds and men and the beasts of the field waited and watched, and the pulse of time was still.

When Sturgess has felt it necessary to abandon all intention of marrying Valerie he walks out with his reflections, and voices them to himself in language that does not carry the weight of its thought:

> He sat down among the trees and covered his face. Memory summoned to him, in disarray, incidents of the days just gone and fragments of them, moods and visions then sacred in their personal validity, presented now as pathetic or absurd, thrown out for the curs of satire to root in: to them the garbage of romance, their natural food. With the eyes of these smart scavengers, he saw his own Unique rotted into their Commonplace, his faith snouted by their avid ridicule. What great words he had flourished then — the very words they mocked at — believing that his own experience was proof against the sneerers at life!

(Is there personal anger here?)

With *A Breeze of Morning*, as lightly composed as an omelet, we are back with prose of the purest Morgan water. The end of the scene of the ball-game:

> ... I prayed all the gods of Olympus to guide the ball into her hands. And the gods knew their own. In triumph, she flung it back at me faster than I could have believed possible, and, the gods being still merciful, I drew it down left-handed out of the air. Backwards and forwards the enchanted ball flew, as it did one day long ago on the shore of the Phaeacians, until at last it went bounding away into the deep, and a thrush came to inquire of the ensuing silence.

In quieter mood and more laconic style, David's description of 'Sundays in my home' — which were 'made to differ from week-days in every way possible':

> We breakfasted at nine, not eight; there was brown

bread, not white, and coffee instead of tea. We all wore different clothes; the maids had prettier caps and aprons and put them on earlier in the day, presumably because little housework was done after breakfast that morning. After midday dinner, at which there was glass and silver not ordinarily used and a table-cloth with such stiff, new creases in it as would tilt a wine-glass incautiously placed, we would spend the afternoon 'basking'. No games were played ... The sewing-machine was put away ... Personal controversy was avoided. 'Six days a week,' my father would say, 'are enough to quarrel in.'

The whole novel is written in a prose that has the limpidity of a Corot landscape.

And *Challenge to Venus* answers to the sun-girt Italian scene and Fiammetta's tropical beauty, with a style that is designedly resplendent:

> Martin ceased to hear Benedetto's voice. He was watching her, who seemed to have emerged from light itself. Her hair fell to her shoulder and curled inward at the base of her throat. Where it lay close, it was of a deep burning gold, brilliant here and there with the high-light gleam of helmets in an autumnal wood; and where it sprang loose, upon her brow and in the narrow diadem of light which encircled her uplifted head, it had the spinning quality of that impetuous spray which runs along a wave-crest beneath an Aegean moon. In her expression, wonder was shot with knowledge, as though for her all sounds were echoes, and by her everything she saw were being newly seen but under the influence of pristine memories.

The many descriptions of Varenna are done in an abundant, joyous, vivid manner.

These pieces that have been quoted are in no way 'purple patches'. They are not much, if at all, above the level of the prose surrounding them. There is hardly a page or a paragraph of Morgan that could not be read as a model for anyone wishing to cultivate that order of style to which Morgan's style belongs — a style eloquent, balanced and shapely, never prolix, rhetorical or insincere, but far from the dry colloquial kind more favoured today. There must, as I have suggested, still be many people with educated taste who prefer a Constable landscape to an abstract painting, and for such people Morgan's prose is full of delight, with its varied rhythms, its ample but never excessive, coloured but never garish, precise but never pedantic vocabulary. It is a style disciplined and graceful rather than athletic, and not violently distinctive: Max Beerbohm would not, I think, have been able to include Morgan in a later *Christmas Garland*. Those critics who turn their backs on Morgan's prose with the one dismissive epithet, 'polished', are those who belong to the generation which believes that some at least of the arts — verse, prose and painting, though music is not yet included — can be practised without the severe training that used to be thought necessary, and which is therefore inclined to be jealous of an artist who has obviously given the passion of the amateur to achieving a professional competence.

Morgan was a great admirer (as who is not?) of the prose of George Moore, but to call him a disciple is to ignore the smiling self-consciousness and engaging bravura of the older writer. Moore and Stevenson (who 'wore his prose with a flourish') illustrate, as Carlyle does in a different way, the 'attitude to the audience' which can be a powerful element in conditioning style. I doubt whether Morgan was even conscious of his audience, except to the extent that he envisaged an audience of cultured people. Having made that choice he wrote to please his own preferences, to satisfy his own exacting standards. Some readers affect to see in this very absence of attitude an attitude of superiority, but we need not take this view seriously. Has it not been observed that most people are alarmed by excellence? The truth is that with Morgan, as with Bacon, Scott, Conrad, 'style lays bare the soul', and those who dislike Morgan's style are expressing a dislike of the man behind the style — and that is their own affair, totally unconnected with criticism.

Let me quote one more passage to show Morgan's prose at its normal level. It is from *Sparkenbroke*: Piers and Mary are in Lucca, alone, after Helen has died and before George comes out:

> To him it seemed that he was discovering her anew. She was young as she had been before her marriage, asking him questions that appeared to spring from ignorance but were full of miraculous, intuitive chances; she was gay and quiet, like the torrent of the Lima which they saw now and then, through the trees, in the valley below. When she put a branch aside and held it that it might not strike him, when she rubbed a leaf between her hands and held her hand to his face that he might have the scent of it, when she sat beside him at a *caffè* and asked suddenly if he could repeat now the lines he had written of Nicodemus, he was enthralled by her. He had not known the lines; now he could speak them as if his handwriting lay before him; and he searched her face, thinking: I cannot lose her; I dare not. The thought, which at first had been no more than an undefined impulse to maintain her in his sight moment by moment, startled him by taking the form of these words: I cannot lose her; I dare not; for thought that crystallizes in words becomes an incantation; it seems no longer to issue from within the mind or be subject to the amendments of reason, it assumes the power of an external command; and Sparkenbroke, wishing by speech to thrust this compulsion from him, said, 'You shall tell me. In what way are you different from other women?'

The passage being read with the consideration it deserves, it is impossible not to be aware of the rhythmic responses to the brief introductory sentence that sets the music flowing like the conductor's baton, each sentence with a different form and its own unique rhythm. The rhythms are those of prose, with no approach to metre (as sometimes in Lamb and Stevenson and lesser writers); everywhere euphony but nowhere melody. And how completely satisfying is the effect of the whole. It illustrates well the qualities

Morgan himself praised in his paper, *On Learning to Write* (*English Association Pamphlet, 1954*), where he recommends as masters for study those whose merit depends on 'the firmness of their line, the lucidity of their expression, and their use of form as a means of fully communicating and lighting their intention'.

It is interesting to note that though in the few poems we have from Morgan's pen in his own name he adopts the undying traditional verse-form by reason of which England has been supreme in poetry for six centuries, from Chaucer to de la Mare, he lets Sparkenbroke use the modern idiom, compressed, contorted, unrhythmic, in the dozen impressive specimens of his work as a poet that are presented for our inspection in the course of the novel. The novel appeared in 1936, the date of the publication of the first collected volume of Mr T. S. Eliot's poems, and Sparkenbroke is supposed to be writing in 1926, just after the appearance of *The Hollow Men*. But Sparkenbroke's verse is not in the least like that of Mr Eliot. It has a certain kinship with the later poems of Mr Richard Church (with a dash of Emily Brontë), but is violently individual, as it were torn from his central self. How different the clear imagery of the calm and moving lines — 'O proud impatient man' — put into the mouth of Julian Wyburton in *The River Line*, and the simplicity of form and diction that clothes the mystical substance of the *Final Retrospect* at the end of *A Breeze of Morning*.

(b) *Diction and kindred matters*

Morgan's diction reminds one of a good plate-glass window: it is lucent and lucid, beautiful, and yet does not draw attention to itself. There is no preponderance of classical words, but equally no trace of insistence on the Anglo-Saxon alternative. Words seem to be carefully chosen but give no sign of effort; they generally have pleasant associations, and they often appeal both to eye and ear. Epithets do not startle by their originality, but satisfy by their appropriateness, and it is not often that a double epithet has to be used to secure exactness. Like the style generally, the diction is idiomatic without being racy, characteristic without mannerisms, excellent without excess.

These observations may be illustrated by a further series of short quotations, chosen almost at random from early, middle and late books, but seeming to contain a number of characteristic words:

from *Portrait in a Mirror*

> Above the poplars the sky swept upward and upward. I let my eyes travel across that washed emptiness whence clouds had sped so fast, leaving no trace but a frozen wisp here and there that seemed engraved upon a glassy dome.

from *The Judge's Story*

> Nevertheless, there closed in about him as he wrote the walls of a room, tranquil and ageless, which excluded all consciousness except of his subject, and, as if the walls themselves were aglow, concentrated light upon it. The intellectual process, which these walls embraced, became intensified to the point of delight; his scholarship began to speak to him with an extraordinary intimacy, to reveal secrets to his intuition which, hours later, his reason tested, to confirm or reject; and he had a sense of there having been made accessible to him a well upon which he might draw endlessly, though he must let down his bucket with as much care and draw it up with as much labour as ever, and be as cautious in his use of what it contained.

from *A Breeze of Morning*

> There fell by chance one of those intervals of silence, rare in the country, most rare in woods, which for a hovering instant awe the mind by their absolute void. Even the small wood-whisperings were hushed; no leaf turned nor twig snapped; there was not the lift of a feather or hop of a wren. A blur of midges swung up and down, into and out of a hard beam of sun, so deepening the silence by the silence of their

fretful activity that there became nothing to listen for except the turning of the earth; but I heard only, deep in my breast pocket, where it hung by a leather strap, my own watch, never before audible at that unfathomable depth, which had begun to tick, with an infinitely remote distinctness, like a huge clock on the other side of the world.

from *Challenge to Venus*

This garden had been no doubt a place of refuge from the heat of the day, but had been designed above all else as a night-garden, not for flowers but for music and lamps. It must have lain, through all its centuries, in a perpetual shade, he thought, unless the turn of the building is enough to admit, at sunset, slanting rays from the west and perhaps a great bar of flame into that projecting turret of hers which she calls her alcove.

I suppose here one must enter a cavil against sundry exceptions to Morgan's usual expert handling of the English language. Most are not worth more than a raised eyebrow — the intrusion of an unnecessary word (e.g. 'a sense of time's candle guttering in her [own] hand'), the use of a pronoun where the name of the person is demanded, twice an uncalled for 'Why on earth ... ' when 'why' would be correct (oddly there is another but different intrusive 'on earth' in *The River Line*: 'Sturgess, who could bath and dress faster than most men on earth ... '), and — really shocking but only too common usage today — 'Beyond the statue ... was a girl whom he did not doubt was Fiammetta.' I am afraid too that one has to count as a fault in style — though one deliberately perpetrated, I am sure — the over-working of certain significant words and expressions, such as *vulnerable* and its derivatives, *bracket* as denoting a piece of time shut off from the rest, *stopping the clock* for a similar idea. All of these belong to important items in Morgan's philosophy, and as such will come up for consideration later, but the use of the actual words should not have been allowed to grow to a noticeable frequency. I have not tried to count the number of instances of the *vulnerable-in-vulnerable* expressions (sometimes in the literal but more often in the metaphorical sense) but they must run into hundreds. Barbet's notion of 'voyages' is again a lovely thing, but the word itself is scattered too liberally through the novel. And sometimes a less significant word crops up with a maddening iteration — *curled* is one in *The Fountain*.

This is to niggle. Let us turn to a more remunerative item, and look at some more of those places where Morgan exercises his special gift of *seeing* the thing that has come in the way of one of his characters. I gave some of these in the chapter on 'action', but many others depend on the choice of vivid, pungent words and visual images. Didn't Dostoievsky say of a penny thrown to a beggar in one of his novels, 'I want to hear that penny hopping and chinking'? It will be a pleasure to quote instances of the penny chinking in Morgan.

It chinks for me in this incident from *A Breeze of Morning*:

> She took my hand and let it go. An instant later she was walking with the others and I was trailing behind them. How cool her hand had been under the lace glove, and how the lace had bitten into me its scarcely perceptible edges, its engraved dryness.

Only style, a perfect choice of words, could make David's intensely personal sensation so alive to the reader. This one recalls another from *Portrait in a Mirror* into which smell, sight and feeling enter:

> The smell was sweet and woody. A leaf fluttered on to my knees which, when I pressed it, stained my dog-skin gloves and gave out a scent as of smoke and violets.

One that includes a marvellous impression of sound is again from *A Breeze of Morning*:

> The gallery was empty and the hall so quiet that a blue-bottle, swinging up into the slack air and angrily swerving

and plunging, made a tearing sound, which dimly reverberated, like that of a string breaking within a shut violin-case.

What brilliance of observation, and of almost onomatopoeic verbal reproduction, is indicated by the words *swinging, slack air, angrily swerving and plunging, tearing sound,* and the final simile, rendering so exactly the minuteness of the reverberating effect.

When Mary is distressfully packing to join Sparkenbroke, 'the tissue-paper surprised her by its whiteness and the fierceness of its hiss'. On the river, when Thérèse lets her hand hang in the water it is Morgan who feels the water 'like a bracelet round her wrist'. When Nigel takes down *Quentin Durward* and stands in his bedroom thinking about Clare — 'my nails were vibrating on the ribbed cover' — it is not just 'a' book but an actual Scott with a ribbed cover that Morgan himself feels under his hand.

To conclude with one or two more comprehensive sense-pictures. Mary, lying in the sand at Chelmouth, remembers the old bathing-machines, and Morgan is instantly there in that bathing-machine, sensing all its 'unforgettable, unforgotten' attributes:

> the gaps between the floor-planks through which appeared the scud of shallow foam, the door-chinks that streaked the floor with pencillings of sun ... the salty smell, the discomfort, the adventure ...

Towards the end of *The River Line*, the others are watching Valerie as her mind moves hesitatingly towards an understanding of her brother's death — and as they watch Morgan watches too, and sees that

> beyond her shoulders a light appeared in Julian's workroom and a small, rounded human figure moved to and fro across the long windows of the bay, beginning to pull the curtains across, hesitating, opening them again, so that the window-beam lay down like a carpet over the steps and the path.

This is not perhaps a matter of style, but of intense visualization; perhaps the same might be said of my last illustration of this facet of Morgan's art, but surely the choice of words and images facilitates communication of the picture: David is in church, Rose and her father are several pews in front, and as he kneels,

> a thin panel of vision, like an arrow-slit, opened up for me on to the Manor-pew, and through it I watched her ear, a lock of hair above it, a fleck of light that moved and danced but settled now and then, when her head was still, in a crescent on her averted cheek; and these things being enclosed, as it were in a frame, which opened or shut with the movement of intervening shoulders, assumed the particularity and the detachment of a fragment of sea-shell looked at through a microscope.

Morgan must have knelt just so and seen such a vision, but what colour-photography of memory!

Another matter not unconnected with style is Morgan's evident fascination by manual and other 'skills' and special branches of knowledge; this I take to be a corollary of his own delight in precision of writing, his own special 'skill'. There is hardly a novel in which we do not find some such 'skill' spoken of and entered into with undisguised pleasure. In *The Voyage* it is the whole business of wine-making, the growth and tending of the vines, the distillation, the marketing —

> The vines themselves were in a condition that Barbet loved. On the main branches the young shoots had grown fast and their green was luminous against the black of the wood. They had not yet spread horizontally and the hoeing was still easy. Tiny green flowers with yellow stamens were opening on the small bunches. From them came a gentle scent, more elusive than that of lime-trees in flower, more delicate than the sweetness of mignonette ...

and the ancient craft of the cooper, his tools and his materials, the mallet, the chestnut hoops, and the paring of the staves, how

H

the clumsy chip-axe must go through the oak like cheese — Barbet felt he would never really master this. In lesser detail we learn about the art of the *diseuse* and the making of her songs; there is also Barbet's knowledge of the way to handle birds; and it is plain that Morgan has sailed a boat. Sparkenbroke, taking Mary round Lucca, suddenly shows an intense interest in and knowledge of the art of the goldsmith and clockmaker: he tells her he hates vague knowledge, and delights in learning the feel of the gold-smith's odd tools, and the dry cedary smell of his workshop, half-way between metal and pencil shavings.

There are other, rather different kinds of skill with which Morgan shows acquaintance, such as the two ways of imparting a knowledge of Latin — by Mr Libbett's method of 'quirks' and cramming, and by the treatment of it as a living language, which is the way of Squire Letterby and Rector Hardy. More than once a character is allowed to expound the finer points of Morgan's own craft of prose; through Judge Gaskony we see the methods of research employed in writing a book on ancient Greece, through Severidge the amusing details of a business man's routine, and through Blachère how to make a bear turn a somersault.

Portrait in a Mirror could hardly have been written without a considerable knowledge of the principles and practice of paint-ing, and through the visit of Jules Coutisson Morgan shows that he is acquainted with the attack of the art critic. But what art critic could improve on the description of Brueghel's *Adam and Eve* as seen by Julie in *The Fountain?* —

> the gracious, smiling countryside that Brueghel had painted, wherein a lion, with grave scepticism, watched the kittenish gambols of leopard and tiger, and all the bright birds, the macaw, the peacock, were showing off their plumage, and the fish, perhaps startled by the yapping puppies at the brink of their stream and plainly determined to be in the picture, were conveniently displaying themselves in water so shallow that it concealed not a scale, not the edge of a fin. Even the owls had kept awake and the tortoise, careless of the guinea-

pigs near by, was making what haste he could into the fore-
ground among the flowers, but not so close to the flowers as
to mask one of their petals or permit them to hide the pattern
of his shell. Only the cats, into whose natures Brueghel must
have had a critical insight, remained aloof, one sleeping
comfortably on the branch of a tree while another, with
happy indifference to the destinies of mankind, was rubbing
his head against Eve's bare ankle while she gave Adam the
apple.

After this it is hardly worth saying that Morgan is interested in
piquet and even in the mystery of cricket, and knows how to
mix an 'old-fashioned' cocktail, but it is noteworthy that in music
he more than once indicates a preference for Chopin because of
his flawless gift of form.

On the whole Morgan presents his novels in the third person,
with 'the omiscient "he"' as the viewpoint. The only exceptions
are *Portrait in a Mirror* (where the power of fantasy is such that
the view is hardly restricted by the narration being given to the
hero) and *A Breeze of Morning*, and since these are versions of
the same story it is perhaps a pity that the second version was not
given a new tilt by being translated into the third person, with the
young man's feelings presented now from the outside. Certainly,
on turning to *The Fountain* after a reading of the *Portrait*, one
feels an enormous gain in having left the shimmering heat-haze
through which the events of the earlier story are seen, to enter
the cold clear air of the external view-point.

(c) *Figures*

Integral with Morgan's style, and an aspect of his poetic
approach, is his use of figures with unusual frequency. In poetry
itself the figure — metaphor, simile or analogy — has at its best
an imaginative and interpretative force — 'All our yesterdays have
lighted fools The way to dusty death. Out, out, brief candle!' —
'Life, like a dome of many coloured glass, Stains the white
radiance of eternity' — 'Even such a shell the Universe itself Is to

the ear of faith'. Otherwise it may institute an illuminating comparison—'Like a poet hidden In the light of thought', or be merely decorative — 'I saw the Pleiads ... Glitter like a swarm of fire-flies'.

Morgan's style does not generally spend time on this last kind. An old couch in George Hardy's surgery is 'perched like an ill-bred dachshund on legs too long for it', and Victor Vincent's feet had no spring in them, so that 'whichever was in the air when he crossed his legs drooped like the tail of a limp cod overhanging a fishmonger's slab'. In the course of a fascinating account of Mademoiselle d'Austerlitz, the receptionist at Barbet's hotel, we are told that 'to any greeting she responded with agitated joy, like a canary when you whistle' (her hair being of an appropriate bright yellow). In the hands of a great humorist the humorous simile can be truly illuminating, as the one Hardy uses to indicate Gabriel Oak's scepticism towards Bathsheba's defence of Sergeant Troy: 'This supreme instance of Troy's goodness fell upon Gabriel's ears like the thirteenth stroke of a crazy clock. It was not only received with utter incredulity as regarded itself, but threw a doubt on all the assurances that had preceded it.' Morgan has to keep that degree of penetration for his graver figures.

There are plenty in the second class, figures that illuminate without being profoundly revealing. Of Julie at night with Narwitz, pitying but repelled — 'Rupert forced up her head, and the boundaries of consciousness rolled back and back in the fierce panic of clouds before a gale.' We understand her state of mind the better for that imaginative analogy; and so with this of the Judge (his money having vanished) looking round at the things in his room in the Temple: he feels that they belong 'to a lost, Arcadian period of his life separated from him by the torrent of disaster suddenly released'. Such illuminating figures are often, like these two, drawn from nature. 'It's quiet in Enkendaal', the old Dutch gardener admits, 'and so quietly did he say it, as if a deeply rooted tree were speaking in the interior of a forest'. And a fact we have all noticed is given a new aspect when we hear that 'some churches, when they are empty, seem deserted and

stagnant ... others are as restfully alive as a summer river continuously flowing'.

A little different is David's brilliant seeing of a 'not-happening'
(something that might have happened had he taken a different
route on his way home) as 'a shining bubble of time lifted away
from me into the air' — one pauses pleasurably on the picture.
And the immortal comparison from the *Odyssey* will always
bear repeating: 'he watched the girl move forward half a pace to
receive her [cup], and thought of a sapling moved by the wind
and straightening itself again.' On the other hand a simile I
cannot altogether approve of is the one that gives us Alison's
reaction to Julie in the early days at the Castle: 'her eyes like the
challenge of a bayonet in a quiet path': danger, yes, but surely
hardness and coldness are implied as well, and these qualities
have no place in the developing picture of Julie. The idea of
danger is enlarged in the metaphoric continuation of the sentence
— 'he was in arms against the invasion of his being', perhaps
justifying the 'bayonet'.

There are two analogies that Morgan is fond of. One is seen
when the Judge, speaking of the new limited life he is about to
begin, says, 'As far as this thing is concerned, I was born yesterday. I have to learn to walk on the waters.' He means of course
that without faith 'the thing' would be impossible. Not only is
the idea used more than once, but Barbet tried it in practice, with
some success. The other is the conception of an episode in life
or in history as being in a bracket. 'This bit of our lives is in
brackets' — and since Alison is speaking of the period of internment in the Fort the metaphor is reasonably exact, though as life
is an organic development it ought not to be possible to feel any
part of it disconnected from what comes before and after. Even
Fiammetta's 'sense of death, of life's being enclosed within the
bracket of a few years', is not quite sound if life and death are
parts of a continuous process.

There is observation, perhaps fanciful, in the statement that, to a
man waking at dawn, 'the morning light was clinging like a mist
to the edges of the blinds'. Of another man who lies waiting in

quiet acceptance for death we are told, with more emphatic fancy yet with an effectual touch of illumination, that to Narwitz the hands of a little old clock, framed by interlaced ribbons of gilt and covered by a convex glass, 'like Chinese eyebrows, stood always at eight minutes to two; and because it had so long ceased to give out any living command or stimulus, it had become, like the face of a priest experienced in confessions, deeply passive, receptive and impersonal'. Mary's description to George of her father raving about her rejection of the eligible Peter is not only couched in unpleasant terms (appropriately so, doubtless) — 'his eyes wide open and the lids white, and his mouth too, like the silvery glisten on meat' — but has also a degree of literary expressiveness improper in the spoken word. But — a really good figure to finish this kind with — we are put fully into George's feelings when, moving eagerly forward to greet Piers and Mary at the garden-party, he sees from their rapt faces that they are in love — 'suddenly he became fixed, the incredible pang struck him, and, observing together the two beings whom he loved best in the world, he felt himself held, like a strangling ship between walls of ice'.

Even the best of the figures so far quoted does not penetrate imaginatively into the essence of the thing or situation described, revealing new truths about it, as do those exemplified from *Macbeth*, *The Excursion* and the *Adonais*. One that has something of this effect, and is indeed a refashioning of Macbeth's thought, is Fiammetta's 'sense of time's candle guttering in her hand', and equally powerful is the one cited in an earlier chapter about desire growing on Thérèse 'like a fungus on the brain'. With force even harsher are the metaphors used, in a passage already quoted, to describe Narwitz's feelings when he suddenly realized Julie's disloyalty: 'He was a child whose mother's breast was entwined with adders; he was the dead summoned to resurrection whose saviour spat upon him and choked him with cerements.' It is perhaps a little too obvious that Morgan has sought for the most dreadful images of tender expectation met by brutal response. A similar objection may be laid against another otherwise brilliant revealing of truth in the same novel: writing to Julie, Alison says, 'There is no surprise more magical than the surprise of being loved: it is God's finger on man's shoulder; there is no peace equivalent to the peace of loving; it is the sigh of a hated child who, laying his head upon his pillow, has consolation in sleep'; I do not understand the need for 'hated' and 'consolation', and altogether the figures are too patently and coldly designed by the machine that is Alison's brain.* Once again, and again from *The Fountain*, I find a measure of unsuccess in the figures used to show the effect on Alison and Julie of Narwitz's arrival:

> They were divided from each other and frozen, every communication suspended, and in each mind was the thought, known to the other, that, though divided, they were bound as they had never been in the past, secretly dependent as prisoners are who in their solitudes tap and tap on the separating wall.

The situation is adequately shown in the first figure, 'frozen, and every communication suspended', but prisoners are not 'bound' by a parting wall, and every communication is not suspended if they can tap. The image of the tapping prisoners is perfectly used by de la Mare in his poem, *The Monologue*, where the separation is not one of spiritual estrangement but of a physical or moral barrier.

It seems that some at least of Morgan's essays in the mightiest analogies of all lend themselves to—probably undiscerning—criticism, and I have one more such objection to bring forward. Morgan's favourite conception, that of stillness of spirit, is in itself metaphorical, and in itself profoundly true. But he more than once tries to illuminate the idea — surely clear enough — by using the old comparison of a wheel, with its motionless centre of whirling activity. But this motionless centre is a point, without parts or magnitude — non-existent. If one must have a mechanical

* Lewis Alison is to some extent Charles Morgan himself. I wonder if this accounts for his being less sympathetically presented than any other 'hero'.

analogy, a gyroscopic wheel seems to me to illustrate stillness that is the result of activity; but surely the perfect image for stillness of spirit is a pool in a stream.

For all my cavils, every one of these striking figures expresses vital truth: there may (or may not) be specks on the lantern's lens, but the light shines into dark places. And there are many others of undiminished force. How better indicated could be the change that came over Mary when she suddenly realized she was in love than by saying 'she was awakened to a second perception of herself, as though she were music that had moved into another key'? What absolute truth about 'book-learning' is here: as Alison leaves the library he delights to think that 'though books were left behind, their wisdom would accompany him and maintain a ghostly world about him, glowing in his spirit as the memory of a summer's day continues though darkness fall'. One of the many problems connected with free-will is almost solved by the analogy (perhaps too profound for Fiammetta) of the stage:

> I don't mean that I hadn't freedom of choice. I could say 'yes' or 'no' as I chose; so could you — so can actors on a stage; there's nothing to prevent them from saying or doing anything they choose — completely outside the parts that have been written for them; but they don't. They speak their parts; they do what it has been designed that they shall do.

The common likening of sleep and death receives a new interpretation when Valerie says of 'Heron's' quiet leaving behind, as he died, of life's effects — 'he let them go, as one lets sleep go when one wakes or lets waking go when one sleeps, easily and simply, without wrench, without loss'.

There are very many other metaphors and similes that could be instanced, for figurative expression is of the texture of Morgan's style and thought: most are highly imaginative and revealing, all add to the fascination of his prose, like the coloured threads in a Highland weave. Other figures matter less. I am not one to look for symbolism, but it is perhaps present in Julie's thought as

— desired by two passionate men — she walks down to Enkendaal: 'She gazed down the great aisle, barred with May sunshine, and thought how exciting it would be to stand like Samson between two trees and break them.'

Irony as a figure — 'that dangerous figure', as Lamb called it — is not much if at all used by Morgan, but there is irony of situation in *Sparkenbroke*, both where Mary is making her first exchanges, at the band-stand and in the wood, with Sparkenbroke without any knowledge of his identity, and where George and the Rector are continuously in Mary's company without knowing that she is already deep in with Sparkenbroke. It is present again in *The Fountain*, where Sophie is painfully trying to screw up her courage to tell Narwitz of Julie's betrayal long after he has known of it and is dying of the knowledge. Bitterly ironic, too, is the scene between Thérèse and Templéraud where she is preparing to surrender her last defences to him — being even willing to burn Barbet's letters — and all the time Templéraud is thinking of Annette, with whom he has already begun a liaison.

(d) *Dialogue*

A novelist's success depends to no small extent on his power to invent dialogue, to make his characters talk in a way that belongs to them, sounds likely, and catches the reader's interest. Likely, but not so likely that you could hear it any day on a bus. How much of the Waverley Novels should we miss without the good Scots cut and thrust of verbal exchange, how much of Meredith without the intellectual fireworks, of Hardy without the immortal rustic chorus; but you would be lucky indeed to overhear such talk even on a bus from Kyleakin to Portree, or in a first-class carriage on the Great Western in the 1890s, or in a village inn eighty years ago in Wessex.

Dialogue, of a sort, perhaps a good sort, is very easy to write —

> "Oh, absolutely,' agreed Harrison. 'Absolutely.'
> 'I see it's annoying for you.'
> 'It could be more so.'

'Oh?'

'It's put me in the way of talking to you — '

just as a photographer with any talent can always make a success with the human face. But to paint a good portrait is as difficult as to write dialogue that shall be credible and yet have the criterion of art, that it shall bear reading over and over again and seem to increase in excellence with every reading.

I think the passage of dialogue from *Sparkenbroke*, at the place where Mary, in Lucca, has decided she must cease to 'lead two lives', fulfils both demands:

> 'This is good-bye, Piers.'
>
> 'Now? Here?'
>
> 'I would rather it were here — on this little pavement — in the street almost. I couldn't kiss you, or touch you, and say goodbye. But first promise me. Promise me one thing first. Let me go. Never find me again. Without you, I can become again what I was.'
>
> 'Then we will go to Pisa,' he said, 'and meet the train.'
>
> 'But first — let me go. Give me your word.'
>
> He could smile now. 'What am I to swear?'
>
> 'Never to come near me. Never to call me.'
>
> 'Such faith in my word? What am I to swear by?'
>
> 'By your work. That all you write may be corrupt and false if — '
>
> His face hardened.
>
> 'Do you mean that? It is final.'
>
> 'I know.'
>
> 'So be it.' And, having said this, he added: 'We are dead to each other. You wished it.'
>
> She nodded, very pale. 'I saw no other way to live.'
>
> 'Then we start for Pisa.' He held out his hand to her and she took it.
>
> 'When I'm gone,' she said, 'you will write your own work as though I didn't exist?'
>
> 'I suppose so. That's part of the oath. The reason of it.'

Tense and terse, revealing, surely 'natural', yet of the same quality as that of the continuous prose of the earlier part of the scene. Are you thinking that the expression, 'that all you write may be corrupt and false', is out of character? But remember this is no ordinary schoolgirl who has just got her G.C.E. at advanced level, but Mary Leward, wife of George Hardy, who has been for long closely associated with the mind of Piers Sparkenbroke, and who was inspired to hear 'the sound of the axe' that set his story of the Holy Face going again.

The *Sparkenbroke* volume is rich in brilliant dialogue. One passage with a lighter touch is that which opens the long and wonderful scene between Mary and Piers in Derry's Wood — she still (at first) ignorant of his identity. The crisp conversation brings the two figures, hardly known yet, before us — he with his mocking but friendly smile and tone, she puzzled, a little frightened, wholly fascinated. Different in character is the talk between Sparkenbroke and George Hardy at the Cottage. George has learnt of the meetings between Piers and Mary, and knowing his friend's ways has come to do what he can to put an end.

'You know,' he said, 'that Mary has broken her engagement?'

'I heard that the youth had gone home.'

'And her father. She's in the devil's own mess.'

Piers seated himself on the edge of the table and threw up his head.

'Is this what you came to see me about?'

'Yes.'

'Well, don't. It's off your beat. It doesn't fall within the category of sins that I confess to you.'

'In a way,' said George steadily, 'it is on my beat. We brought her here. She's our guest at the Rectory now. She was Helen's pupil. What's more, we're fond of her, and she — she's in a very deep confusion.'

'Is she? George, you're making a very great fool of yourself. You'd better come away from the fireplace —

standing there, warming your moral coat-tails, doesn't become you.'

George tried to smile. 'Very well ... Very well,' he said awkwardly, swerving before ridicule. Then he went on: 'She's been here often?'

'You know that?'

'Yes — in fact — I do. She told me.'

'Then you needn't have asked.'

'Does Etty know it too?'

'I'm sure she does. She has an intuition in that. Her only one.'

'Piers, you say damnable things! They're not the truth of you.'

'Then why in God's name invite me to say them? What are you? The Mother Superior of this girl's convent? Or my wife's confessor?'

The grim scene continues, George's plain honesty barely a match for Piers' bitter wit till George, not caring now, cries,

'And is she also part of your necessity — a drop in your waterfall, like your art and — '

'Go on,' Piers said.

'And your tomb.'

So George wins his point and Piers scuttles off to Italy. Not all the dialogue in this novel depends on Sparkenbroke. There is a long talk between George, as medical adviser and friend, and Lady Sparkenbroke on her health and her relations with her husband and George's opinions and Sparkenbroke's art — full of half-confidences and searchings of heart: every exchange is a personal contact, and yet one realizes what made George wonder, as he took his leave, 'whether even her solitudes were armoured'.

The Voyage is remarkable for the two hugely funny figures of the two elderly mothers, Chouquette Hazard and Emilie Vincent, and there is some amusing dialogue between them, as well as a talk, half-humorous and half-pathetic, between Thérèse and

Madame Vincent, whom Thérèse has picked up, exhausted from the streets of Paris, in her carriage. But serious conversation, discovering the roots of things, is Morgan's province. In the last pages of *The Judge's Story* Severidge has come to Gaskony's poor lodging in Margate, and having failed in his last temptation is about to depart, as the Judge repeats,

'Do you understand that, Severidge? I am happy as I have never been.'

'In your book?'

'Not even in my book. That may or may not be the flower of it. The root is in my life here — in myself, and beyond myself.'

'Am I to believe that?'

'Is it so hard to believe?'

Severidge picked up a sheet of paper from the table and let it fall. 'While you stand there, it is not hard to believe', he said reluctantly ... 'But the more I believe that you are not lying, the less I bow down to your truth. The more I believe you, the more I hate and despise you. You are an accepter of life, I am a rebel against it. Why has man no courage? Why does he not rebel? The flower is always poisoned — do you never suspect the root? Even in Athens the flower was poisoned and died.'

'Ah, Severidge,' the Judge answered, standing at the open door with him, 'It's not in Athens that you will teach me to despair. No one learns to hate life in the early morning.'

'As far as human life is concerned,' Severidge replied, 'I make no distinction between morning and night.'

'That is the answer of the dead.'

At this Severidge, whose foot was on the stair, swung round, his eyes alight, but the words that sprang up in him were unspoken.

Here the dialogue, though easy and rhythmic, is obviously polished, epigrammatic, too good for normal improvised speech, but the interlocutors are both in their way intellectual giants, and may be allowed to express themselves in memorable terms. It is otherwise with Thérèse and Barbet, when, after Barbet has escaped from prison, they sit in Thérèse's bedroom and talk in long elaborate paragraphs absurdly beyond the bounds of verisimilitude. And Venetia is once made to talk to Richard Cannock as if she were Sludge the Medium. But these lapses are rare.

Besides dialogue brilliant or intellectual, Morgan can do the other kind — there are conversations of the plainest order in *A Breeze of Morning* between David on the one hand and the Squire or a railway porter on the other, and never a pointless or wasted remark — no 'ohs' and 'absolutelys'. Mr Letterby is trying David out at their first meeting on a piece of Vergil:

> ' ... Go on, if you can.'
>
> But Mr Letterby had the text; I was remembering. ' "And her hair," ' I began again, ' "breathed ... breathed out the scent of heaven" — or something like that, sir, isn't it?'
>
> 'Something very like that,' he answered with a sigh. 'Now, tell me, why did you mark that? Why is it likely to be "given"? Anyhow: "given" in what, may I ask?'
>
> 'In my scholarship exam.' And encouraged first by his questions, then by his attention, I told him my trouble and my fears. I told him even of Mr Libbett's quarrel with my prose. 'You see, sir,' I explained, 'he's frightfully hot on Cicero. He always says: "Cicero wouldn't have written that," and I can't say back to him "But Tacitus might have." Even if I did, he'd only say: "You play safe. You stick to Cicero. Then as far as the Examiners are concerned you can't go wrong." He always says that. And then he says: "It's just a question, Harbrook, whether you want to get that scholarship or whether you want to show off." '
>
> 'And which do you want?' Mr Letterby inquired with a shrewd glance ...

There is no falling off in *Challenge to Venus* — in the conversations between Count Ascanio, with his witty but shallow cynicism, Sullivan the sage or wise Maria Guerini, and Martin or

Fiammetta; all fascinating though a trifle more 'literary' than usual.

> 'You are peaceful to be with,' she said (it is Fiammetta to Sullivan).
>
> He wanted nothing better, and had no impulse to answer; but in order that there should not be a tension in their silence, he said: 'Well, you see, I watch life from the bank.'
>
> 'And rescue the drowning?'
>
> 'Not,' he said, 'officiouslly to keep alive. It's for them to sink or swim. But if they climb my bank, I don't push them back. I give them time to breathe.'

It is another side of Morgan's art, and one that gives immediate pleasure, this power of writing dialogue that is never stilted, but easy, natural, alive, and characteristic of the people speaking, yet full of significance and on the level of literature; and if it be objected that such conversation is not common, one can only reply with Turner, 'Don't you wish it were!'

PART III

The Philosophy of the Novels and Plays

CHAPTER ONE

General

'Ez FER my principles', said the Parliamentary candidate, 'I glory in havin' nothin' of the sort', and a novelist will feel the same way about his 'philosophy'—if he is a 'pure artist', like Scott and Jane Austen. But pure artists are rare in prose, and Arnold thought that even a poet should have a 'message' (though his own poetry is as free from adulteration as almost any). Hardy was angry with those who tried to deduce a philosophy from his 'impressions of life', but we have insisted on doing so, especially as he packed his verse with unabashed 'philosophy'. I think it is permissible, even desirable, for an artist — certainly a novelist — to have conceived a way of life, to have drawn a few tentative conclusions from experience, and if he embodies them in his work we may call them his philosophy; and if he is a true artist, 'pure' or not, it will be worth our while to pay some attention to what he puts before us. We are first to enjoy a novel, just as we are to enjoy living, but if we do not learn, as Butler said, the instrument of life from playing it, we ought never to have taken it up, and we should (generally) learn something more about life from a novel we have enjoyed.

Unfortunately a 'philosophy' is not now reckoned as of much account unless it is founded on 'disillusion', depressing and depressed. Has this writer, they ask, compassion — for sinners, for sufferers, for mankind? He surely must have compassion for mankind when it suffers and sins, but he may feel able to congratulate mankind on those considerable periods when it is not thus wasting its time. Has he tears for mortal things? they ask. Yes, but smiles too. Has he a sense of man's predicament in the universe? May he not rather have a sense of the adventure? Morgan's philosophy is not a tragic one. He presents life as a judicious mixture of sweet and bitter, with not more of the bitter ingredients than will serve to make the sweet the sweeter. I should not be writing this book if this outlook did not give me much satisfaction.

The difficulty about the philosophy of a novelist is that most of what we have to go on consists of the opinions and conduct of his characters, with comments of his own interspersed. But with certain novelists, of whom Morgan is one, many of the characters — easily distinguishable — represent aspects or facets of his own mind. Just as the four persons of *The Excursion* — Poet, Wanderer, Solitary and Pastor — all stand for various sides of Wordsworth, so Morgan has put something of himself into Nigel Frew, Lewis Alison, Piers Sparkenbroke, George Hardy, Barbet, Rydal, Judge Gaskony, 'Heron', David and Christopher Terriford. Each of them exists in his own right, but each also stands for an outlook on life that belongs to Morgan. What they say and do can, with caution, be taken to indicate something of what he thinks and approves of.

Beyond this, and perhaps more acceptable as a measure of Morgan's philosophy, there can always be found, for each novel, an idea on which it is based. Such basic idea is conceived, not in the abstract, but as a human situation: Morgan has never lent his name to the *roman à thèse*. He has been accused* of 'working problems of art and morality into his novels with a relaxed dexterity' (I suppose the last phrase means 'effortlessly'). Morgan's novels are concerned with such problems, as are the novels of George Eliot and half the novels that have been written since, but the problems arise quite naturally out of the action. And all the problems, all the separate lives and embodiments of this conception or that, are but leaves floating on the surface of the all-embracing, all-compelling idea which moves for ever through Morgan's imagination, giving ground and substance to his fiction: the idea of a deeper Platonic reality, the vision of a greater life to which mortality blinds us, which we can conceive, approach, enter into by achieving a certain stillness of soul, whence, by wonder,

* By Mr David Daiches.

by contemplation, by art, by love we 'see into the life of things' and become as gods. This is how Morgan apprehends the universe, and we become bigger by sharing his apprehension.

I said above that each of Morgan's novels and plays is founded on a basic idea, just as each of Shakespeare's plays (at least of the tragedies) has a 'motive'. I imagine every reader will perceive a different basic, but for what they are worth I give my own readings.

> *Portrait in a Mirror*: the conflict of art and love.
>
> *The Fountain*: contemplation and love.
>
> *Sparkenbroke*: the place of sex in art.
>
> *The Voyage*: love's acceptance, and the necessity of freedom.
>
> *The Empty Room*: love and forgiveness.
>
> *The Judge's Story*: the contemplative life as a defence against evil.
>
> *The River Line*: stillness of soul in a world of violence.
>
> *A Breeze of Morning*: beauty as a symbol of divinity.
>
> *Challenge to Venus*: the pride of beauty and its dangers.
>
> *The Flashing Stream*: singleness of mind.
>
> *The Burning Glass*: the madness of excessive power over nature.

CHAPTER TWO

Religion

Of all the elements that make up Morgan's world, organized religion is the very smallest. There are but two representatives of the Churches. One is Rector Hardy, as wise and delightful a man as one could wish to meet in a day's march, but evidently one who looks on his churchmanship as a minor issue. (His son George, no less good and wise, is a confessed sceptic — 'theologically'). The other is the Roman Catholic priest who is father of Thérèse — brooding pathetically on his daughter, tormented by futile remorse, strangled by inhibitions, offered as a contrast to the happy and mildly Protestant Barbet. There is a little ineffective English church-going, Judge Gaskony says his prayers — standing, in his pyjamas — 'Lighten our darkness' and 'Make me fit to write'. David, who depends on his gods and his magics, once prays (lying in bed and staring at his drawn-up knees) for deliverance for himself, Ann, Rose and Howard. *Challenge to Venus* gives us a charming picture of a convent school, showing how a religious discipline may be cheerfully accepted and made to bear fruit.

The only indication that Morgan took any interest in the teachings of orthodox Christianity is the prefixing to *The Empty Room* of some stanzas from Blunden's *Report on Experience*, suggesting that evil, in the form of the affliction of innocent men and women, is God's 'curious proving that He loves humanity'. One has to be very far gone in orthodoxy really to believe this, believe it with understanding, and it may be that Morgan quoted the poem only for the sake of the stanza about Seraphina, who, however, does not stand very exactly for Venetia in the novel that follows. Perhaps another indication of the sort is Christopher Terriford's calling in of St Luke to support him — or rather

Mary — in their stand against the extension of power over nature.

For the rest, we are in a secular world, if by secular we mean outside the institutions of religion, the Churches and their elaborate doctrines. But only the shell of religion is institutional, and if by religion we understand a sense of God, a living relationship with the unseen, a spiritual vision of man and the universe, then the whole system of thought that permeates the Morgan world is religious. There is not one of those characters who were said to represent aspects of Morgan who does not live by the sense of God in one form or another, whether it arise from art, imagination, wonder, peace, love, magic, humility. To Sparkenbroke imagination is the evidence of God, the Kingdom of God within you. For Narwitz God's own essence is an infinite power of wonder, and wonder is man's highest faculty — 'all the judgments of morality and philosophy are fused in wonder'. Barbet, who is too busy and practical to have much use for mysticism, one would suppose, is yet aware of the continuity of time and the unity of all being. His 'voyages' are an acknowledgment of the directing finger of God: they mean the time has come for a new way of life. Judge Gaskony realizes that he is not too old at sixty-five for such a departure and the faith it needs. Rector Hardy's version of the 'voyage' is that to every man there comes at least one moment when the gods offer him a chance of changing his nature and becoming — perhaps a saint. David is genuinely in touch with the unseen through his magics. It is imagination and humility that lead Alison and Narwitz to accept Turgenev's suggestion that 'to put oneself in the second place is the whole significance of life'. Alison carries the idea further by asking what is to be put before oneself, in the first place. The Christian answer is God; Alison suggests Art or God; Narwitz asserts confidently that 'Death is the answer'.

There are many doors into the unseen world of reality, and the key that fits most of them is the artistic imagination. The poets have always believed that imagination is something more than fancy. Coleridge expounded the supreme creative power of imagination, which enables the poet to grasp the unity of life and the nature of God. Keats was certain of the truth of imagination. Morgan began by showing, in *Portrait in a Mirror*, a belief in the high vision of visual art. Art in later novels means poetry, prose, contemplation — the last enabling us to bring in Barbet, David, 'Heron', Gaskony, all of whom are poets in spirit. Art is 'the most profound of all the intimations of immortality', and gives us eyes to look up and down the river of time. Man has two spiritual impulses, to penetrate reality and to be permeated by it. Sparkenbroke has two convincing images of how art can show us reality. He says the walls of life go up unscalable, but can be made transparent by 'poetry, music, mathematics, all the supreme exercises of human perception'. At another point he is trying to explain to Mary what he feels to be 'the continuous meaning and purpose of life'.

'Look,' he said, with new eagerness. 'I can tell you a little of what I mean. Do you see the windows of this room?' She looked towards them. 'The curtains are back. What do you see?'

'Nothing, it's dark outside.'

'But outside are the garden and the ramparts and, above the ramparts and between the trees, the whole sky lighted up. There's nothing between us and them but glass, and glass is transparent. Now, tell me again what you see.'

'Only the glitter of lamps and candles on the pane.'

'They are this world. While they are shining in our eyes, we can see nothing beyond them. Put them out, and suddenly the night and its constellations rush in; all its distances are within reach. That is what happened in the Mound, and why I am drawn back to it. And there are ways,' he said, 'while we live, if not of putting the candle out, at least of hiding it a little while, in love or poetry: every man has his own way, according to his nature and powers; they are imperfect, but they are all we have while we are shut into the lighted room. In death, I think, the walls go down, the lights blow out; that is all, for death is not a change of state but a change of lodging; it is an incident in a continuous immortality.'

And from the story of Nicodemus he draws the esoteric definition, 'All perfect art is a likeness of God carved by himself in the sleep of the artist', recalling Nigel Frew's declaration that 'everything is made in sleep'. (I do not understand these two assertions, but they should be acceptable to the current belief in the 'unconscious'.)

To Barbet imagination was a practical instrument. He believed implicitly in its efficacy, but distinguished a false kind from the true, 'which falls like the touch of a hand on one's shoulder and is certainly fulfilled'. It enabled him to trace the lost Thérèse, and showed him at last that he must free his prisoners and emancipate his soul. Let us pause to note that the power of the imaginative life in no way detracts from the life of the senses. The miracle of earthly life — which can be clear and delicious as a meadow stream — is given full recognition, if nowhere else, in *The Voyage*. Barbet, enjoying a day on the river, remembers another of long ago, 'as full as this of breeze and sunlight, with the same tension of the body, the same taste of life upon the lips'. It is Barbet's mother, dying, who says, 'When you grow old, Thérèse, do not say goodbye to the nightingale.' David sees the personal life, 'life itself', as 'something quite simple and cool', and his innocence and classically brightened vision make *A Breeze of Morning* a monument to living beauty.

Yet always one has the feeling that for Morgan's people it is that other life that is supremely important, 'life external to the body'. Sparkenbroke hears continually 'the rumour of a life not yet attainable'. Even substantial Barbet is aware, 'if we could feel it', of a comprehensive continuous life beating like a pulse beneath the individual life. We find even Martin Lyghe at one point thinking of 'that timeless world, beyond the window-glass of temporal existence, of which, since his childhood, he had been intermittently aware, as we are of the constellations beyond the room in which we sit'. This echo of Sparkenbroke must be deliberate, an attempt to redouble the force and impression of that most illuminating analogy. Later Martin reflects, in Brontëan terms, on the way in which the vision was accompanied by 'a bliss and agony of isolation'.

We are approaching mysticism, that mysticism which, in a novelist, is a stumbling-block to the reader who prefers such things to be kept for the text-book and the treatise. (As a matter of fact, in most of the novels and plays after *Sparkenbroke*, mysticism is present, if at all, in unobtrusive form, and 'won't bite'.) The reader who is an amateur of mysticism enjoys a novel that makes play with the possibility of mystic revelation, just as a member of the Alpine Club enjoys a novel about mountaineering. That there is nothing professional or exclusive about the mysticism of Morgan's novels is shown by the fact that one of the best accounts of mystic experience is put into the mouth of the airman Herriot, who tells Alison that he flies 'for the sake of the flash of seeing that comes now and then — almost as if one died bodily, and escaped from oneself and saw out on the other side'. He calls it an 'exaltation', and says that if Alison can achieve such moments 'the thing ... will be the whole of life to you. Sometimes you'll call it God, and sometimes you'll feel that it's nothingness...In what way you'll reach it I don't know. Maybe through solitude. I doubt it. I believe you'll find what you are looking for *in* the world, not in withdrawing from it'. Herriot's is the way of the sudden vision induced by experience at an unusual tension. Alison's is the traditional way of contemplation, and though he felt that 'to identify the contemplative with the mystical purpose would be to identify a mountain with one of the many streams that sprang from it', he 'began to think of contemplation as the crown of all men's hopes'. For contemplation can be not merely a means to occult knowledge but a way to the good life. Certainly the vision and the grace are not restricted to men of contemplative genius. It is Philip Sturgess, ex-American soldier and now college lecturer, who, inspired by an unselfish and apparently hopeless love, watches Valerie for her beauty, and, as he watched, there came to him from within her an interior grace, hers because she was the lamp that gave it out, yet not hers only. Of this enduring light, seen through men and things, and yet not part of them, as light is not part of a lamp, he became aware through her, who was alive and within reach of his hand, as he had been aware of it a few hours earlier through Heron who was invisible; and for an instant the distinctions between physical presence and physical absence were burned away in his mind, and creation shone singly. Even when the experience again receded from him because he was not trained to accept it and grapple it to him, the sense of it remained in his sense of its having passed, as though he had touched the hem of a garment.

The mystical condition most characteristic of Morgan's thought is that of quietism, the word being used here with the modern everyday significance and not in the technical sense of *Inglesant* and the Molinists. Nigel is telling Clare he may fail to achieve success or fame, and when she suggests, 'Perhaps in the way you live you will be great', he wonders if she fully intended 'that superb philosophy of quietism'. The special words associated in Morgan with quietism are 'citadel' and 'invulnerability'. 'Contemplative stillness [it is Alison again] is but the name for a state of invulnerability.' It is 'an exercise of the imagination which enables a man to live within his own citadel of values while material values perish'. It is 'stillness of soul' (reminding us of Wordsworth's 'happy stillness of the mind') that is perhaps seen in Richard Cannock's thought that for spiritual despair there was 'no remedy but quietness of spirit, for to the spirit that is quiet a natural refreshment comes as to a body that sleeps'. Akin to this was the relief brought to Julie's tired mind by her viewing of Brueghel's picture in the gallery at the Hague, making her feel that 'works of art that men love are a cloister where they may have absolute retirement and a cooling of their fevers in the world'.

Generally we are dealing with something more permanent,

more integral than this. 'Absolute stillness of the spirit' is the result of perfect tension, and can be attained only through a singleness of mind of which Barbet Hazard alone among Morgan's characters knew the secret.* And this was perhaps due to his acceptance of life — 'how to live simply and with acceptance so that no work of men shall have power to separate me from the peace of God'. Judge Gaskony excited Severidge's hate and contempt in that he was (or had learnt to be) an 'accepter of life', and certainly no man can know happiness and peace without accepting life as good. However, the condition of mind we are examining is not of one kind only. Nigel Frew saw rather than realized it as a consequence of the artistic vision; for Sparkenbroke it resulted from a passionate longing for death; while it came to George Hardy out of his firm hold on life. Barbet's approach was to stop arguing and go on and on: 'to accept life in this way, not to force it, not to plan it'; though he knew that only within himself were such acceptances possible. 'I intend', he tells Anton, 'to lead my own life in my own way ... living patiently as regards others and accepting what they do ... I want to keep my mind clear, that's all, Anton.'

Discipline is required to achieve stillness, but the asceticism enjoined by the text-books is firmly ruled out. The ideal is to discipline but not annihilate the senses. I have already pointed out that there is no absence of sensuous delight in these novels (quite apart from sex). From some points of view, and particularly from that of the first half of the Twentieth Century, perhaps the sanest attitude to existence is that implied in Barbet's observation, 'A June morning, and no war!' Carey knows something about this: 'There are days when everything glows and shines, special days — the air smells different, even a horse you meet looks different and somehow benevolent.' Maria Guerini, whose lovely wisdom is Morgan's best argument for the religious life, tells Martin, 'Seeing, physically, with my eyes, has always been a supreme pleasure for me.'

* In the foreword to *The Flashing Stream* Morgan tells us he wrote the play as an act of refreshment from a novel that was coming with some difficulty, its theme being singleness of mind, and a comparison of dates shows this novel to have been *The Voyage*.

Though the life of the senses is an unending miracle, the miracles most associated with Morgan are those happenings of an improbable or unpredictable sort which produce a result that seems to have purpose behind it, and which almost presume a power operating beyond the senses. Of this supernatural or fantasy element enough has been said in an earlier section, and more interesting at this point is the importance attached to the greatest miracle of all, the miracle of identity or personality.

One of Morgan's favourite questions is — Who am I? who are you? — an inquiry drawn directly from Plato, and more profitable than the Victorian whence and why. It is asked first somewhat naïvely by Nigel Frew as he reflects upon the love (only exceptional in that on his side the worship of beauty is involved) that is springing up between him and Clare: 'But who is she and who am I that in our mutual love I should see the origin of love and a beginning of the world?' To which echo might answer, 'Who indeed!' David, Nigel's younger stand-in, asks exactly the same question, but more idly, less pretentiously, yet with deeper suggestiveness: as the mystic feelings associated with the ball-playing scene begin to fade, David muses, 'Lyric and elegy are one. The shadow of her head is lengthened upon the grass. The thrush is gone. Hail and farewell! Who is she, after all? And who am I?'

But the exploration of the significance of this question comes in *The Judge's Story*, with *The Voyage* the wisest and most satisfying of the novels. First the Judge considers it in a general way: he is wondering at his conduct over the wager and at what he is having to do to get out of the pit: 'Good God! That's how my mind works! — "Know thyself", said the Greeks.' Later both Severidge and Gaskony are found confronting the problem (and we have been told earlier that though Severidge could always find an answer to the question, 'What do I do?' he could find none to the question, 'Who am I?'):

> Severidge said, 'At this moment I seem scarcely to know who I am or why I am here.'

'That is what I am learning,' the Judge said.

'What?'

'Who I am — why I am here. There are receding answers to those questions. Gradually one comes up with them.'

But it is Vivien who is to be saved by being compelled to face the question. She, who has been so strong in her resistance of Severidge's temptations, is now in danger of yielding, and has come for help to 'Gasky', who has, till now, been so weak. She is bewildered by Severidge's kindness and considerateness, by his flattering pretence that he 'loves' her; she is on the brink of accepting his luxuriant 'love' in preference to the simpler love of Henry. Her instinct has already whispered the critical question to her: 'When Severidge, helping her into a cloak, let the back of his hand rest, and move, upon her bare shoulder ... her body said to her: Who are you?' And now she is drastically put through it by the Judge. To her complaint that she is 'tired of saying What shall I do?' he answers that she must 'learn to be. Learn that and nothing can touch you, neither authoritarianism nor the devil himself'. Still she is inclined to believe that Severidge is kind and good. 'I think he's honestly fond of me — and of you.' The Judge quotes Satan from *Paradise Lost* at her, and she sees his drift, but says, 'Tell me, not in Milton's words but in your own, what I am to do.' ' "What I am to be" ', the Judge said, correcting her [again]. 'What I am to be. Who I am', she answered.

So he brings her, by a Socratic interrogation, to realize there is 'a principle of individuality — an essence without which you would not be — at the heart of your individuality' — 'an Absolute You as there is an Absolute Beauty', which is the answer to the question, Who am I? an idea that is always 'alive in you, deeper than thought, deeper than feeling, the very spring of instinct and intuition, the original, the unsilenceable whisper of the soul'. He is teaching her to look at herself objectively, to feel and know her 'self', and he completes the instruction by telling her:

> 'You aren't your intelligence. You are your whole self — the infant you have forgotten, the child you remember, the

old woman you will be. You are the girl who saw that life was good, believed it with a single heart, and began to doubt it with a divided intellect.'

Vivien's reaction is to long for Henry to come and take her home.

It would have been well for poor Mary if she had had counsel of this sort as she waited for Sparkenbroke on that terrible last evening, thinking, 'Who am I, standing out here in the night?' Whether or not George was able, like Gaskony, to teach her (and George and Gaskony were two of a kind), we may be sure Mary learnt the answer for herself through the long years of happiness with George.

In the last of the novels the exposition of the mystery of personality is given to Sullivan, who alone can persuade Fiammetta to 'listen like a three-year child'. She has asked what he means by speaking of her 'identity'.

> He paused carefully. 'Not soul or spirit, and not character; something distinct from both. What I mean by Identity is probably what you mean when you speak of the 'feel' of a person ... A man has a soul or a spirit. It isn't separate from the body. All the same, before the body was, the spirit existed, and after the body has gone back to earth the spirit will continue ... Then there's something about a man or woman that we call character ... to be read in behaviour and appearance. Identity isn't. It isn't observed; it is felt — or not felt.'

And he tells a story of how the 'uniqueness' of an apparently harmless stranger's 'identity' once put his bristles up and made him run away. I take it the terms identity, individuality and personality are names for the same mysterious essence of a human being. It is the strange interplay of three identities — of Valerie, of 'Heron', of Sturgess — that gives the last Act of *The River Line* its power. It was to this mysterious essence in David Harbrook that Rose's beauty appealed, as he told Ann by saying she 'worked his deep magics'.

There is in Morgan no serious suggestion of 'fate', so conspicuous in Shakespeare, Hardy and Conrad. (And he makes Marie Wyburton say she is sick of the quotation, 'The President of the Immortals had ended his sport with Tess.' She felt it was so small a part of Hardy.) The nearest he comes to it is in a suggestion that 'life' may take a hand in bringing things about: Nigel Frew, at the end of his story, reflects that now it was not man or woman that there was need to fear, 'but rather life's reluctance to complete the pattern of personality, its tendency to leave you encumbered with dreams'. Which is only a way of shifting responsibility off one's own shoulders. In *Challenge to Venus* 'fate' is playfully impersonated in 'the gods'. Sullivan quotes, *Nemini divos licet aemulari*, and applies it, with some cogency, to Hitler. Later he elaborates the thought (with special reference to Fiammetta but with the same historical application): 'The extremes of power or genius or beauty seemed always to breed in their possessor a pride, hubris, distinct from vanity — a sense of special privilege, of exemption from the divine wrath visited upon excess.' This is fate endowed with eyes and brains, an aspect of man's (perhaps inspired) 'invention of a God of morality'.

In the preface to *The Burning Glass* some views are expressed on 'Nature' which may have been adopted for the purpose of the argument against the growth of scientific power, but which, if intended to have a general application, are not very philosophic. There is an elementary personification of nature, to whom is attributed a compassionate and ironic eye, and who is presented as threatening to abdicate in favour of man. Even more doubtful is the personification of evil. We are to 'acknowledge a Satanic principle and design', and see that design 'persuading' men to abandon the anthropomorphic name, Satan, in order the more thoroughly to get itself accepted. I find this odd, in an adult thinker.

It would be hard to say whether the quality of a religious philosophy is better tested by its attitude to life or to death, but every important attitude to death gets its expression in Morgan. To Sparkenbroke death was an ecstasy, the supreme art, the one completely safe and certain way of achieving full knowledge of reality. He was impatient of the idea that 'death is, as it were, an unwarrantable interference' — or, as Courcelet thought it, 'an embarrassing solecism'. The will to death implied no hatred of life, but induced a greater sensitiveness to all that is meant by being alive. Death was not a change of state but a change of lodging; it was an incident in a continuous immortality.

Narwitz believed that while he was lying unconscious on the island, he had visited the kingdoms of death, and afterwards he had a desire not to lose contact with this supreme experience, hungering for the new life as an exile for his own remembered country. He had been changed by his experience, and the warmth of the change was in his soul 'like the sun in an apple yet upon the tree'. His desire for death was 'an eagerness for the perfecting of the contemplative life'. 'It seemed to him that he lay in a womb, eager for the summons to birth.' He died crying, 'Into thy hands I commend my spirit.'

All of which is paralleled on a simpler level in the account of the death of Barbet's mother, which comes to us largely through the eyes of Thérèse. She sees in Madame Hazard's state of mind as she draws near to death 'an extreme simplification of life ... a reliance upon nature and upon a goodness inherent in it* ... She neither clung to life nor clamoured for death, their continuity having appeared to her'. An occasional word came from her lips: 'After all, there is nothing to be afraid of.' 'You mean in death?' 'I mean — in life'. And just before she died, 'When you grow old, Thérèse, do not say goodbye to the nightingale. It is not necessary.'

For 'Heron', we can only judge by what those who killed him saw in his eyes as he died, nothing dark, but 'light and light-bringing' — 'loss without losing'. There is great consistency about all that Morgan has to say and show concerning death.

---

* Cf. A. N. Whitehead, 'a reliance that fine action is treasured in the nature of things'.

CHAPTER THREE

Morality

THE TERM 'morality' implies the acceptance of rules of right conduct and the judgment of conduct according to its concurrence
with or divergence from those rules. On the whole such standards
seem to play little part in the implied judgments that Morgan
passes on his characters. We know he approved of the man
'Heron' not because he is described in the last passages of the book
as a loyal officer but because to meet him 'gave a lift to the heart
like food or wine'. When Morgan's people do right it is not
because they have been taught the difference between right and
wrong but because their instincts are for rightness. Vivien seems
to be devoid of the moral sense that would have enabled her to
estimate Severidge for the evil person that he is, yet at each point
where she is in danger of surrendering to him, an intuition wakes
in her and she is at once safe. Conversely, it is not Thérèse's
conduct as a prostitute that condemns her, but her lack of the
instinct that should have made her turn from Templéraud as
from a nasty smell. Instead she 'loves' him passionately, and for
him she would have burned the unopened letters of Barbet. Yet
her relation with him is artificial and confused: she lies to him
out of pure wilfulness, whereas, as Courcelet tells her, she would
never lie to Barbet. The criterion implied is a sound one, and is
that put forward in a pronouncement by an anonymous French
thinker: 'There are many philosophies, but only one morality,
namely the power of distinction between the beautiful and the
ugly.' This makes morality a branch of aesthetics, a place it had
already been given by Ruskin: 'Taste is not only the index of
morality. It is the *only* morality. The great question is, What do
you like? An act is not right and proper until it is liked.' How
well Morgan understands this view of morality is shown by some

146

emphatic words of that exquisite figure of the background in *The Voyage*, Madeleine. Speaking about her lover, Cugnot, to Thérèse, she says, 'I don't make sacrifices for him. If I did, I should think I was ceasing to love him. What others, outside, would call sacrifices are nothing of the kind. They are a part of loving him.'

Yet we are not allowed to feel that the aesthetic criterion excuses conduct that is obviously wrong — for example, cruel. Sparkenbroke's search for women who shall quicken in him the urge to artistic production is seen to be at least tainted with self-indulgence. At one point Morgan seems to fall a victim to the antinomianism that is the danger of this position: he describes Sparkenbroke's face as having the character 'that appears some-times in the young men, at once spiritual and dissolute, whose vitality shines down from the canvases of the seventeenth century'. If the dissoluteness was real, i.e. involving cruelty, meanness, pride, the spirituality must have been the invention of the artist. I suppose we have here a reflection of Dostoievsky's elevation of spiritual excellence over moral: all I insist on is that the excellence should not be bogus. Shaw presented a similar view — not too convincingly — in the sponging artist in *The Doctor's Dilemma*. We are on surer ground when we read that Sparken-broke felt that when he was writing he was without evil: to imagine was absolution, to be putting imagination into words was innocence. Or is this too but the dual nature of the artist?

The aesthetic approach to morality is the most promising one, as Wordsworth admitted even while he was invoking the God of Duty:

> There are who ask not if thine eye
> Be on them ...
>   love an unerring light,
> And joy its own security.

But some grasp of moral principle would surely have saved Alison and Julie from blindness to their appalling treachery to Julie's husband. Love, they protested, is no sin — but an oath had been broken and a faith betrayed. It was not so that Augustine intended his tremendous aphorism, 'Love, and do what you will.' Julie was troubled by bitter qualms of conscience, not because Narwitz was her husband but because he was a great man, and when Alison at last came into contact with him he realized painfully the nature of their action. This is reasonable: just as to kill a good man is a sin whereas to kill a very bad man may be no sin at all, so with betrayal — except that the act of betrayal, irrespective of its object, has in itself a corrupting effect on the soul of the betrayer. Morgan makes his view of the conduct of Alison and Julie clear (if not perfectly clear) in the only artistic way possible — by showing them unhappy and confused after Narwitz's death.

On the other hand, a man of happy instincts, like Barbet, is able to ignore the sound principle of truth-telling when he feels that a lie is required to restore an old lady's ease of mind. It is Barbet too who knows that it is not conduct but the spirit of life that counts — not what people do but what they are. That Thérèse lives the life of a prostitute does not please him, but it is as a woman that he loves her. What Severidge actually achieves of harm does not amount to much, but his whole life and personality are black with evil intent. He is a sentimental hypocrite; would wish, even as he spreads his nets and plans the degradation of society, to do no one any harm. Morgan's stand on moral questions can be deduced from the fact that, as he clearly loves Barbet Hazard, so he obviously detests Severidge.

In one striking instance Morgan takes — or allows one of his characters, a good and delightful woman, Mary Terriford in *The Burning Glass*, to take — a very 'realistic' view of moral action. At the opening of the play we see her permitting Tony Lack to make love to her, simply because the only way to stop him would be to inform her husband, in which case there would be a quarrel followed probably by Tony's losing his post. Mary does not want either of these things to happen, so, as no one is being hurt and Tony is being pleased, she lets the love-making go on, though receiving it with the proper degree of rebuff. At the end of the play she sees, in a mirror, that Tony is putting poison in his drink and committing suicide. Again she decides that it is Tony's only way out, and does nothing to stop him. The assumption is that a rational adult has a right to freedom of action, including the disposal of his own life, provided his action does not harm other members of the community — and in Tony's case it did not. The position is tenable, though arguable, but here again Mary probably acted on a true instinct rather than on moral principles. I am afraid less can be said for the other Mary when she lies to George: he has been expressing his concern at her visits (the early ones) to Piers at the Cottage, and when he asks if these visits really must be continued she says,

> with a quick radiance of compassion: 'Not if it means so much to you', lying to him as she would have lied for the immediate consolation of a haunted child, but lying also with that spontaneous and intuitive subtlety of women which, when passion is fallen upon them like a hood of light, enables, and indeed compels, them to divide their enchantment from their experience, and to deny the truth of their character that the truth of their instinct may be preserved.

I do not well understand this, but it is a fault in Mary that she does nothing about this promise but break it.

There is just one condition that exempts from the demands of morality, the condition of extreme beauty, which may be 'beyond good and evil' — 'its beauty its sole duty'. Rose Letterby and Fiammetta are a-moral. Rose plays with Howard's heart and Ann's happiness as a cat plays with a bird. She gets as far as telling David that she feels 'half-false' in everything she does, but the passing thought skims lightly over her conscience, and she goes beautifully-dutifully (and as it turns out harmlessly) on her way. Fiammetta's a-morality arises from the equipoise set up by the interaction of her heredity, she being the daughter of a vicious mother, and her training at the hands of the pious Genevra Valmontana. At first the results of this training are all-powerful: she appears self-disciplined, devoutly Catholic, proud, and her life is rational, wholesome, virtuous. But this does not constitute her 'morality' — it is a covering of brittle clay banking in the furnace of desire which, her innate self, blazes forth when the proximity of Martin Lyghe cracks the shell.

To repeat and elaborate an observation made earlier, I think Morgan's attitude on right living and wrong living is shown by his loving treatment of those of his characters who live beautifully and his manifest distaste for those whose lives are ugly. Not all novelists are thus discriminatory. What feelings, for or against, had their creators for Becky Sharp, Steerforth, Stephen Guest in *The Mill on the Floss*, Sergeant Troy in *Far from the Madding Crowd*, Irene of the *Forsyte Saga?* Criticism generally approves of the impartiality. Does the fact that Morgan is (in my view) less impartial make him less of an artist? I do not think so. He takes as much delight in the limning of a Victor Vincent as in that of a George Hardy, but as he contemplates the result he cannot — I believe he should not — resist a curl of the lip over the one and an affectionate smile for the other. And it is a good thing that the feeling should come through to the reader. We are never aesthetically-minded without qualification, and a sound moral sense need not spoil an artistic gift. The brilliant art of Restoration comedy might have given even greater aesthetic satisfaction if it had had behind it the moral sense of Shakespeare.

With Shakespeare goodness is beautiful; with Wycherley and Congreve evil is charming; with Morgan, though we are often asked to accept artistic integrity for moral excellence, the other side gets fair play. In *Sparkenbroke* it is put bluntly in the person of Peter Darkin:

> Mary said quietly: 'I meant — only that you hate poets'.
> 'Nothing of the kind. They make no odds to me'.
> 'But you resent genius, Peter. A lot of men do. It's a kind of bad form, isn't it?'
> 'What I resent,' he said, 'is your idea that because a man can write he can behave as badly as he pleases and get away with it.'

Puritanical, low-brow, bourgeois? But not nonsense. The answer to Thérèse is Barbet, and George is the real knock-down answer to Sparkenbroke. That people like Venetia, Fiammetta, Mary, Gerry Hardlipp should be regarded as not fully responsible at the bar of morality is presumably a matter of less importance in these days of a fading belief in the freedom of the will, but thinking men and women are not thus absolved, since conscience is a function of intelligence. And if this is so, it should be possible to forecast consequences and so avoid the error Alison and Julie had to admit: 'It is the consequence that matters, not the intention ... The sin, though it seemed not to be a sin, grows to the stature of what we sin against.' This pragmatic approach to morality is dubious: by it, if Narwitz had died before coming to Enkendaal the sin, having no consequences, would have been no sin. And perhaps it would not.

The basis of conduct at its best and surest would seem to be the Wordsworthian impulse, an instinctive rather than the reasoned source of action that was so emphatically recommended by Socrates. It is to be noted that Julie's instincts were all against developing the affair with Alison. There is a form of acceptance more ethical than the spirit of acceptance considered in the section on religion: it is shown in Barbet — our exemplar — 'To accept life in this way, not to force it, not to plan it, but to accept it.' And he knew that if the 'realities' of the world were to be overridden it must be 'not by any act of will but only by those impulses of nature which, like the touch of a wing on the surface of a pool, trouble the water and send out rings endlessly.' Courcelet — whose great merit is that he loves and understands both Barbet and Thérèse — reflects that 'It was the essence of Barbet's nature that he lived by no rules and yet had order within him, the order of ... his own sense of natural values.' It was this principle that lay at the heart of that expression so often, in one form or another, on the lips of both Barbet and Thérèse — When you are ready, you will know what to do. Barbet once tried to apply the magic formula to Lancret, but the priest could only half accept it for himself, though he commented that 'a man in doubt must believe that or perish', and pointed out that 'that promise, like every other, is in the gospel itself: Knock and it shall be opened unto you'. To which Barbet might have replied, 'Knock, then, and be at peace.'

Martin Lyghe's 'abrupt certainties' fall under this head, but the most interesting extension of the idea is to Vivien's instincts in *The Judge's Story*, already mentioned. Over and over again, when her reason, fallible and at the mercy of Severidge's cunning, told her he was 'kind and good', an intuition saved her and enabled her to say *Retro Sathanas*. As the Judge told her, she is not her intelligence but her whole self, and instinct or intuition must be explained as a reaction of the whole self to a problem of conduct, other forms of sanction being to intellect or emotion only.

With Morgan's emphasis on spirit one might have expected his philosophy to lean towards asceticism, but this does not happen. We have already seen Sparkenbroke and Alison deciding that the life of the spirit can and must be lived without hatred of the life of the senses. The two lives are not lived in separate compartments. Martin Lyghe believed that 'the pleasure of the body has, for good as for evil, its projection in the spirit, as suffering and cruelty have, and all the seizures and submissions of the flesh'. George Hardy is less interested in the question than most of his fellow-characters. Talking to Lady Sparkenbroke he admits that he has 'very little sympathy for the sins of the flesh. You see, I happen not to be tempted', and explains this as fidelity to the memory of a lost love, but really it is 'the way he is made'. Like Barbet, he knows 'the sins of the flesh were not the ones Jesus condemned'. Lancret the priest cannot accept this. When Barbet suggests that Thérèse is not 'proud or cruel or mean or cowardly' — the sins of the spirit — the priest cries, 'You don't understand what she has *done*!' and Barbet replies, 'We don't yet know what she is.'

We have impressions of intense pain in Sparkenbroke and Narwitz, but the experience is not shown as having any educative value, and Sparkenbroke's heart goes out to one who is 'young and not in pain'. Pleasure, on the other hand, is seen by Courcelet as a good because it is a means of communication, and Thérèse declares the art of life is to waste the instants that are too precious to be used. Indeed, Morgan values the beauty of civilized life, its culture and its manners, as highly as Galsworthy valued that lesser thing, 'good form'. Dick Gaskony, the Oxford don, was puzzled that the Athenians produced so great a civilization on such poor wine. Every novel has a background of culture and graciousness, and even the Judge would not have accepted what Dr Lin Yu Tang calls 'financial competence with a pinch' if he had not known it was to include access to that noblest of civilized institutions, the public library. And there are always the primitive pleasures, 'the enchantment of being alive' which Martin Lyghe knew as he came out of the shadow into the benign warmth and brightness of the full morning sunshine. It was from the insight of mysticism that Tagore wrote, 'I will never shut the door of my senses. The delights of sight and hearing and touch will bear thy delight.'

A special moral theme examined in *The Voyage* is that of the ethics of imprisonment. Quite early in the story we find Barbet troubled by a problem he has 'not yet enough simplicity to solve', though since he has none of 'the self-consciousness of power' his position is not, we feel, doing him positive harm, though he feels that it is he himself who is imprisoned. Yet it is only under Blachère's gaze that Barbet is 'vulnerable', and he afterwards feels sure that if he had not solved his problem in the way he did, he could not have retained his integrity. But the ethical dilemma is presented as it affected Barbet, not in a universal frame. When Thérèse first suggested to Barbet that he should set his prisoners free it is on the grounds that 'they are men', and it would be at least a permissible reaction to this to ask what sort of men. It is strange that it is the evil of Blachère rather than the harmlessness of the other prisoners that eventually turns Barbet's mind in the direction of a decision.

I have said that Morgan does not preach. Yet what a sermon could be made out of that last talk between Vivien and her beloved guardian. Even to be with him lifts life for her on to a more significant level. 'Your fortress isn't mine, I know; everyone has his own if he can find it; but at any rate you make me feel that I have one, and that life isn't an anonymous, meaningless drift.' Taking this up the Judge shows her that she must not divide her forces, must beware of the devil, and be her single-minded self. She is to obey her own instincts, but they must be the instincts of her whole self, so that Vivien 'begins to feel again the singleness of her girlhood that had been confirmed and deepened during the early years of her marriage'. His steadiness gives her peace, and when she leaves him she is free of Severidge's devilish power for ever.

Morgan's moral values are based on a belief that life should be lived abundantly, completely, beautifully, without codes or inhibitions. There is no recommendation of this virtue or that, as fidelity with Conrad. Avoid the joylessness of a Lancret, the meanness of soul of a Victor Vincent, the malice of a Severidge, he might say, and shun materialism like the plague — otherwise live to the full the life that is in you. And don't be bound by custom — always be prepared for a 'voyage'. Judge Gaskony, wisest of Morgan's men, reflects thus:

> Is any man too old to accept, with joyful equanimity, a revolution in his life? — then he is already dead. Is he too stubborn and fearful to be reborn? — then he is a clothes-prop, a dummy of the armchair. Is he so wrapped in custom that he cannot strip and be his naked self — then, in himself, he exists no longer but is of the mass, the mob, the ugly and nameless proletariat of the soul.

CHAPTER FOUR

Love

THE EXPRESSION 'sacred and profane love' has been used more than once in earlier chapters, and it is time we had some explanation of what meaning the expression is intended to carry (whatever Titian — or his interpreters — may have meant by it). To speak of sacred and profane love is merely to say that there are two primary forms of love, each doubtless with a dozen or more varieties, and neither necessarily superior to the other: one, passionate, but quietly passionate, bringing lasting peace to body and spirit; the other based on violent desire, disturbing, in itself short-lived. The former kind is the natural basis of marriage, the latter is generally that romantic love which has produced most of the world's great love-poetry. It is romantic love involving violent desire that is characteristic of Morgan (though in point of numbers just as many of his people experience the quieter kind), and in his writing it is associated with a mystical conception of sex. It is more than once associated with 'the bliss of nakedness', and Ferrers tells Karen Selby that when, on the first day of her joining the unit, she stood before him, he saw 'a woman naked'. We find this kind of love exemplified in Nigel and Clare, Alison and Julie, Sparkenbroke and Mary, Martin and Fiammetta, Ferrers and Karen. Whether you find the permeating atmosphere of hungry sex — morbidly worked up in *Portrait in a Mirror*, desperately satisfied in *The Fountain* and *Challenge to Venus*, frustrated in *Sparkenbroke*, taken for granted in *The Flashing Stream* — whether you find it compelling or distasteful, depends partly on whether you were born after or before the turn of the century.

It is only in his exploitation of the mysticism of sex that Morgan has any kinship with D. H. Lawrence. The theory of the matter is expounded succinctly in *Challenge to Venus*, where we read that,

> Raised to the degree of ecstasy, physical passion shared is an emptying away of time and circumstance, a self-abandonment to a plane of consciousness where other selves lie in wait ... No one emerges from it unchanged ... Its effect upon one sharer in it may be radically different from its effect upon the other. Upon one it may leave the hood of madness, raising to the degree of obsession the appetite it appeared to statisfy; and yet, in the other, be illumination.

(There are echoes of Sonnet 129 here.) Elsewhere (and not only in Morgan and Lawrence but in sober spirits like Shaw) it is said that such passion opens the eyes to a miraculous vision and understanding of natural and other beauty and truth, and if one complains that one sees small evidence of such vision and understanding the reply comes that the passion envisaged is rare. Or Patmore may be right —

> Love wakes men, once a lifetime each ...
> And some give thanks, and some blaspheme,
> And most forget ...

In a review of Miss Dallas Kenmare's book, *The Philosophy of Love*, 1942, Morgan wrote, 'Pleasure, considered as part of love (and he means the pleasure of the sex-act) awaits its metaphysician.' To some extent he seems to intend Alison and Sparkenbroke to be the oracles of the metaphysics of sex-pleasure.

The two foci of Alison's thinking are contemplation and sex-love. When he is brooding alone — before the meeting with Julie — on the latter he seems to me to drift into wild nonsense: he passes from 'the Elizabethans' exquisite insanity of passion' to the thought that 'men, being children first and last, see their god through women, and have no peace but at the breast and no imagination of rebirth but in the similitude of a womb'. After he and Julie have become lovers his feelings are saner — a poetizing of desire; he can recognize that the bodily delight of love becomes a deadly betrayal when a human relationship is obsessed by it. Sparkenbroke has even greater powers of self-analysis and lyrical expression. He explains to his wife that love is for him 'not affection only, however profound, nor passion only, but an ecstasy, a dying to be reborn', and he too is capable of seeing this as 'an insane egoism'. He longs to 'love absolutely', but pins his faith on sex. He seems incapable of learning from those moments when, with Mary, lust is forgotten in a diviner force that merges into art, and she inspires him to his work. Sparkenbroke's fatal fallacy is his belief that women exist to provide a means for the 'release' that shall set the artistic impulse free: 'no one loves a woman for her own sake only — because she is she'.

> Because by passion I am made her child
> Whom, till she love beyond passion, she bears not,
> I must subdue her as though she were a slave.

It was to refute this 'insane egoism' that Morgan created Barbet Hazard (the refutation having been insufficiently effected in the over-reasonable and uninspired person of George Hardy). And it is to be noticed that if Barbet represents a saner variety of love this may be partly due to the fact that he has something more to do in life than brood on his desires. It is also to be noticed that Barbet gives as one of his reasons for loving Thérèse that she 'opens windows for him' — a quieter version of Sparkenbroke's demands, and achieved without any sex-mysticism. Thérèse is undoubtedly the better woman for Barbet's love: one cannot say the same of Julie and Mary. Thérèse can see and talk plainly: 'I wouldn't [formerly] admit that anything in love was more important, more real, than that hunger [of desire] ... I am going back on my old creed. It was much easier to be a plain hungry animal than to love a man as I love you.' And how the ravings of *The Fountain* and *Sparkenbroke* fade into a whimper at the sound of her lovely conclusion:

> 'Barbet, remember sometimes that I have not the consola-
> tions of philosophy. The reach of your hand is that to me —

even if you are too far away to touch me. When I believe you love me, I am proof against all fear, temptation and loneliness. Only give me evidence sometimes that I am in your heart.'

And it is Thérèse alone who diagnoses true love by her instinctive realization that she and Barbet are 'the same person' — a fact that was recognized about themselves by Cathy and Heathcliff, by Jude and Sue, by Robert and Elizabeth Browning. (Venetia claims, but sentimentally, that this is true of her and the husband she had deserted for the prosperous retailer. Anstey, too, in Morgan's radio play, *The Confession*, with perhaps more plausibility, feels it was true of himself and Sylvia.)

This more rewarding love, operating under difficulty in George Hardy, and springing into being full-blown in *The Voyage*, plays its part in the stories of Sturgess and Valerie, Cannock and Carey, Christopher and Mary Terriford, Howard and Ann, Vivien and Henry, and perhaps Cugnot and Madeleine, and — in a different way — in the love of Will Gaskony for his lost Julia and his ward Vivien. David's love for Rose belongs of necessity to this second order, but, by reason of his belief that he was aware of the goddess behind the mask of beauty, shares in the mysticism of the first. There are signs that Julie might have preferred to continue in the 'deep companionship' of her early relations with Lewis. As Morgan insists that there are women like Karen Selby, who live in the desire for men, we may allow Shaw's suggestion that there is among women a tendency to share Julie's dream. In *Getting Married*, Mrs George, a woman who has plunged deep into the life of passion, says that perhaps the thing women want most is something the priest might call 'Christian fellowship'. Hardy made Sue Bridehead speak of 'the wide field of strong attachment where desire plays, at least, only a secondary part — the part of — who is it? — Venus Urania'. This of course is Victorianism, and probably irrelevant to the new knowledge of love vouchsafed to the Twentieth Century. But it is legitimate to wonder which of the two loves, 'sacred and profane', presented with such impartiality by Morgan, and yet with a subtle emphasis on the 'profane', fits in best with that love which Diotima told Socrates would bring him in sight of absolute beauty; to wonder which of the two Aldous Huxley had in mind when he said that 'to be in love is, in many cases, to have achieved a state of being in which it becomes possible to have direct intuition of the essentially lovely nature of ultimate reality'.

We do not take Courcelet very seriously on vital matters, but he speaks with his own sort of knowledge when he tells Thérèse that it is best to be sensually mature before falling in love, because 'love is an art, and an amateur does not produce an enduring masterpiece' (how many masterpieces did Keats have to produce before he ceased to be an 'amateur'?). More interesting is Martin Lyghe's realization that he would not have loved Fiammetta at all if she had not been beautiful: he loves her for what she is, but would never have 'learned to see within her except by the light of her visible glories'. And there is a wonderful definition of love (George Hardy's love) in *Sparkenbroke*. Mary is resting in his surgery, and George, watching her, is filled with 'that emotion towards beauty which, projecting the beholder into the timeless essence of the beauty seen, creates in desire the illusion of immortality, and is called love ... George was at peace, his longing for her quieted in a passionate tranquillity'. The use of the word 'illusion' in reference to desire points straight at one kind of love, and the last two words at the other — a diagnostic of love as experienced by George and Barbet. There is an 'invulnerability' in love of this kind, and this implies loving not being loved. Severidge was all at sea over this as over everything else that matters — his wish was to be loved. Thérèse, in spite of her amatory vagabondage, never really ceases to love Barbet and in consequence is fundamentally undisturbed by either Courcelet or Templéraud. Barbet is invulnerable in this respect as in all others. Vivien, loving Henry, and disappointed at his not turning up miraculously, as Barbet would have done, is able to say, 'It doesn't matter. It's as if he had.'

Marriage is not the necessary end of love in Morgan. Barbet

and Thérèse are very clear on this — that not every pair who love ought to settle down together for life. Narwitz argues the unbreakable solitude of the individual mind, even love — 'a form of suffering' — giving but an unreal semblance of union. But Narwitz has never known returned love, and is steeped in suffering. Helen Hardy 'thinks of marriage as if it were friendship', and though eternal friendship makes a good marriage (it made a good one for George and Mary once Piers was dead) Helen can only know marriage from the outside. More interesting is David's suggestion to Ann — in the epilogue, forty years on — that the mutual chiming of the spirit implied in his words, 'she had the power to work my deep magics', might have provided a basis for marriage (Ann thought — for love only). Sullivan, out of a long, observant life and a wise head, told Martin 'marriage doesn't work unless both people believe in the marriage with their minds as well as with their hearts', which must be true, but he hesitates to add that marriage is not a lyric but a narrative with a beginning, a middle and an end. I am fascinated by the glimpses we are given of Alison's first love, Elizabeth, and I feel she might have made him a more satisfying if less exciting wife than Julie.

There is one other theme in the love-symphony that Morgan treats with almost mystical feeling — the theme indicated by another of the Sonnets — 'Love is not love That alters when it alteration finds.' There is no length to which forgiveness and understanding are not to go. George Hardy begins it: he shows no sign of even resenting Mary's broken promise not to visit Sparkenbroke again at the cottage, or her unmistakable fascination by his rival. Barbet utters no word of complaint about Thérèse's disgraceful behaviour: she is, he believes, unchanged in herself by what she does. Moreover, the theory is that when a man settles to love a woman he accepts everything she has done and may do in the future. 'Forgiveness after the event doesn't amount to much. Love begins at the beginning, that's all.' Rydal is the chief exponent of this theory. Venetia has left him for a man who is a figure of fun, but when, years later, Rydal finds her, with brandy-tippling added to her infidelity, he takes her clean back into his love. She is more embarrassed than surprised. 'The whole point of Henry,' she explains to Cannock, 'is that he ever-lastingly re-imagines a woman he loves; it's his way of loving her; he isn't the kind of fool who ties a woman down to one set of facts.' Carey feels she herself cannot swallow this — 'what Father calls "the principle of love" — the power to love *through* criticism, to recognize vileness but not to be dried up by it'. I don't think the story quite stands up to the principle — it does not convince. It is interesting to find this same exalted idea of forgiveness, indeed the same situation, in the radio play, *The Confession*. Again Anstey, after many years, finds Sylvia (who has, he believes, deserted him for Hugh) in poor circumstances and wants her back, wiping out all memory of what she may have done to him. It is remarkable, too, that in this last story occurs the first mention of jealousy. Love in Morgan is free from low emotions of this kind. Ned Fullaton perhaps shows a trace of it, but it was not jealousy that lacerated Narwitz, nor do we see it in any later man or woman, however deeply wronged, till we hear Anstey con-fessing, 'Jealousy, fear, anger — that's what broke Sylvia and me.'

Benedetto at first finds it hard to forgive Fiammetta. His face contorted, he cries, 'You should not have come to me. You should have gone to a priest ... for absolution.' But before the end he has effected the miracle: 'His eyes were already wide open to Fiammetta's wickednesses. He didn't have to forgive her for them; he didn't even have to shut his eyes to them. He saw them and saw through them — and loved what he then saw.' Only your 'profane', romantic, mystical lover is unable to rise to these mystical heights of forgiveness, which indeed demand a self-abnegation that runs contrary to the whole principle of his being. Sparkenbroke explains to the Italian doctor: ' ... if she betrays him, though he can pardon her and perhaps desire her again ... he cannot, in the same way, love her again. She has destroyed an idea, and ideas have no resurrection'. And pop goes mystical love — it is love not for a woman but for an idea.

In spite of — perhaps because of — Morgan's preoccupation

with love and its dominating position among the motives of his novels, it is not to sit at his feet that I would send a youth or girl seeking instruction in the ways of love before entering the labyrinth. Meredith and Hardy might be found less confusing, though of course the poets are the safest guides, for while the love they write about is romantic love, all true love must begin as romanticism.

CHAPTER FIVE

Women; Politics; Humour

(*a*)

THERE IS a great deal to be learnt about a man by noting the position woman takes in his mind and conversation, and there is something to be said for judging the quality of a creative writer by the way he handles women in his work. If one were to adopt this criterion, Shakespeare, Scott, Browning, Tennyson, Hardy, Meredith, Barrie would come out well, Milton, Fielding, Dickens, Thackeray, Conrad less well. And Morgan joins the second group. He is in no sense a feminist (not that I am suggesting that all or any of the members of the first group were feminists). Occasionally one notices a sentence with a slightly condescending air about it, as when Alison thinks to himself, 'Many women are like stringed instruments; they respond to a touch, and we suppose that they have music in themselves.' That Sparkenbroke regards women as material for his art is a reflection on him, not on his creator. When men get together in Morgan they talk of women as if they were put into the world for no other purpose than to satisfy men's desires, but this is simple realism.

More instructive is the obvious fact that in practically all the novels and plays the outstanding figures are men. They leap to mind — Alison, Narwitz, the Baron van Leyden, Sparkenbroke, George Hardy, the Rector, Barbet Hazard, Judge Gaskony, Ferrers, Christopher Terriford, the Prime Minister. Only in two novels is the centre of the stage held by a woman (rather, a girl) — Rose Letterby and Fiammetta, and perhaps Valerie Barton takes this place in *The River Line*. In *The Judge's Story* Vivien is a better horse than Henry, Marie in *The River Line* perhaps than Julian, Mary Terriford at least as good as Christopher; and I think we are to admire Julie more than Alison. But to balance this,

Barbet is made of far finer stuff than Thérèse, and Nigel than Clare. The thought comes that Venetia is the poorest character in Morgan, whether one regards her as bad or weak — and then one remembers Victor Vincent, beside whom poor Venetia is as silver to lead. At one point we hear that 'Women worth having are drawn to austerity in a man', at another we are dismayed by the spectacle of Thérèse being 'drawn' to Templéraud (as Bathsheba to Troy and Eustacia to Wildeve in Hardy). Julie is one of the finest of Morgan's women, yet she feels that both Narwitz and Alison have the power and right to 'transmute' her. With all Etty Sparkenbroke's dislike of her husband's erotic adventuring she yet regards him as a god.

If it is legitimate to look at an artist from this particular angle, there is no doubt as to how Morgan comes out. It may be that the attitude to women — what shall we call it? — superior, patronizing, or simply male? — that appears from the inspection is a corollary of the mystical feeling about sex that we have found permeating much of Morgan's work. Even to conceive the idea that woman may be a means by which man achieves a desired condition, physical, mental, spiritual, however exalted, must be degrading to the mind conceiving. In Morgan the result, without being that, is that only a few of his numerous women and girls — Valerie, Marie, Vivien, Ann, Mary Terriford — can stand as entirely worthy of the men who love them.

This view of women, if it was Morgan's, is a much diminished relic of the Nineteenth Century attitude from which Charlotte Yonge could say, 'I have no hesitation in declaring my full belief in the inferiority of women.'* It was an inseparable factor of a man-made world, and is as strongly held today by the 'common man' as ever, being (like the colour-bar) felt to be a matter of self-preservation. But most thinkers on the higher levels now accept as axiomatic the complete equality of women, and imaginative writers like Bennet, Wells, Shaw, Forster and Priestley have played a helpful part. And by 1953, in his last full-length production,

---

* Quoted by Miss Naomi Lewis in an article on women in literature in the August, 1958, issue of *The Twentieth Century*.

The Burning Glass, Morgan had reached a point where he could create the marvellous figure of Mary Terriford, the most complete woman in his gallery, a full atonement for all the earlier faint disparagement. I shall have more to say about her presently.

(*b*)

Mrs Morgan has called her husband a 'Royalist-Romantic'. We are all royalists, but the term, as applied to Charles Morgan, is more comprehensive than its reference to the head of the state. Morgan, like Walter de la Mare, Mr T. S. Eliot and others for whom culture is inextricably involved with means and privilege, did not find the social and political changes that have come about since 1918 much to his liking. This, however, is made apparent chiefly in his essays, and rightly allowed to have little effect on the fictional works.

I do not find any specific political references earlier than *The Empty Room*, where Rydal is made to express a proper realization of the fundamental difference between the First and Second World Wars, the Second being 'a religious war'. On narrower lines, Rydal and Cannock are said to love England in the same way — 'that is, in the light of her continuing destiny, for the sake of her continuing people' — a sound sentiment which may be Toryism writ large, just as it is possible to spy imperialism in Rydal's later remark that 'for years politics has consisted chiefly in ... cutting down the trees — beginning, for choice, with the branch your own country is sitting on'. In *The River Line* observations of this kind are given to a strong-headed old lady, Mrs Muriven, who (reasonably enough) demands that the Western democracies should accept their responsibility for dealing with the barbarians. Marie presently puts this into very definite terms:

> The herd-peoples are still moving westward. Twice the flood has been thrown back. There is a third to come. The extreme Right and the extreme Left, the men of blood who,

under different names, are entered into the same conspiracy against us, do not die. They wait their time.

When Judge Gaskony couples authoritarianism with the devil we know (from the essays) that Morgan is not thinking only of the dictatorships but of tendencies nearer home.

The most interesting political thesis is the one specifically put forward in *The Burning Glass*. It is hinted at in *Challenge to Venus* where Sullivan says 'men's sin in the modern world consists in their having become too big for their boots'. This unnatural and uncomfortable growth has taken two forms, political and scientific. It is the problem of what to do about the scientists' determination to use more and more of the powers that lie hidden in nature that is handled dramatically in *The Burning Glass*, and I propose to examine it in a special study of that play. Morgan's fear that we are 'subverting the natural order' by gaining power *over* nature seems unfounded: man is as far from controlling storm and earthquake, hurricane and flood, even ordinary 'weather', or any of the vagaries of nature as he was in the Middle Ages. On the other hand, in view of the accumulating evidence of the stupid uses man is making of the new powers he has acquired, I find it a little pathetic that Morgan should have felt, in 1953, 'a stirring of dread in the world', if he meant an *effective* stirring among the people who rule us and have the control of these things in their hands.

(*c*)

Some men have no sense of humour but are incredulous and annoyed if you tell them so. Morgan almost boasts of the deficiency, and claims it as a strength. It is not that he has no gift in humorous writing. Think of those two exquisitely funny old ladies, Chouquette Hazard and Emilie Vincent, and their fencing matches — there is as much humour in their presentation as in Mrs Poyser. And there are a few happy moments elsewhere— one of the best at the end of *The Burning Glass*. After all the melodrama, the moral arguments and the momentous discussions the Prime Minister is going up to bed. As he crosses the room he sees a half-finished game of chess set out, and stops by it.

> Now, tell me, what would happen if White moved his Bishop — there? Seems the obvious move, am I right?
> *Christopher*: Well, yes, except that it isn't White's move.
> *Prime Minister*: What? Bless my soul ...

The form of humour called satire generally distorts, and Morgan seldom indulges it. A pretty example, gentle enough, is in *A Breeze of Morning*. David, in the punt, is brooding, when 'Miss Featherford astonishingly spoke'.

> A deep brown voice beside me asked whether I was fond of strawberries, and I saw that Miss Featherford was wearing a huge garnet-ring on her right hand. The garnet recurs much later on the gunwale of another punt sliding past our own, and again at supper. With that Miss Featherford vanishes, to become, I believe, an ambassadress.
>
> Nevertheless I still recall my grateful feelings towards her. She was precisely the kind of woman — girl, I suppose, by the counting of years — who has always paralysed me. Gruff, cheerful, slangy, a gusty talker about dead birds, dying fish and alive horses, she seemed to wear leather where others of her sex wore ribbons. I was not even shy of her, so remote from me did she seem, and had been completely unaware that she was beside me. I assumed that we were as far apart as an Eskimo from a Hottentot and that communication between us was impossible in the nature of things. For all the initiative I should have taken, we might have been silent through eternity on a desert island. No doubt she was as little interested in me. But she troubled to ask whether I liked strawberries and whether I didn't prefer horses to motor-cars, and listened to a reply inevitably voluble and almost certainly, before it was done, Hellenic. She had breeding and suffered fools officially, as an ambassadress should; and she was kind. Of such, when the gods play the game, are the kingdoms of this world.

A neatly executed vignette that might have come straight out of Mr Harold Nicolson, and of which there is no other example in Morgan.

But it is against that sense of humour which prompts a man to see a comic element in a serious situation and hence to treat it less seriously that Morgan brings his indictment in the Essay on Singleness of Mind prefixed to *The Flashing Stream*. He refers to it as 'that acidity of derision and self-derision which is mis-called 'a sense of humour', and he complains that it is an enemy of singleness of mind. In the play Ferrers is the single-minded and humourless man. I suggest that Ferrers would have been a bigger not a smaller man if, recognizing the Admiralty's difficulty, and (as Butler recommended) denying Christ for Christ's sake, he had been able to say with a smile, 'Error? All right, have it your own way. Let's get on with the job', and so got on with it, instead of forcing Karen and the First Lord to supply his lacking sense of humour and make the little concession between them.

In the Essay Morgan goes on to spoil a perfectly good case by over-statement. For singleness of mind is a noble and necessary factor in human activity: it means that once you have decided that a course of action is right you must pursue it without being deflected by seeing other sides — including a funny side — to it. But a sense of humour will save you from pursuing it past the point where it ceases to be good to do so. Chesterton was a great humorist, and a very wise man. It was, I suppose, his sense of humour that allowed him, wise as he was, to join the narrowest (though not the most humourless) of the creeds. But I do not believe he ever allowed his sense of humour to turn him aside from any of the causes — mostly splendid, a few less admirable — that he had at heart.

PART IV

Individual Studies of the Chief Novels and Plays

CHAPTER ONE

The 'Sparkenbroke Trilogy'

THERE IS a definite break between the first three novels and those which followed. These first three, *Portrait in a Mirror*, *The Fountain* and *Sparkenbroke*, all have behind them a speculative theme that was clearly much in Morgan's mind during his fourth decade but does not recur after 1936 — the significance of art and of love, and the relation between them. I speak of 'the *Sparkenbroke* trilogy' because that novel alone presents with completeness the thesis embodied in the action of the three novels, without in the least weakening their narrative force. Nigel Frew, Lewis Alison, Narwitz make their contributions towards it, but Piers Sparkenbroke knows with fullness and certainty what these others were feeling their way to. And we know that Sparkenbroke's dominating conception was not given to him by his creator merely as part of the mechanism of the novel of which he is the hero. That it represents something vital to Morgan himself is shown by his own statement to George Moore that three things interested him above all others: art, love and death; and that he thought of them always as three aspects of the same impulse, the impulse to recreate oneself.

This conception is the soil out of which the shapely tree of the trilogy of novels grew. In love, in contemplation (the mystic contemplation that issues in art), and in death, man hears and understands the language of the gods: these are three ecstasies that are one ecstasy, three deaths that give entrance to life. Death is the common term, the type of all three achievements, the symbol of new life. Sparkenbroke tells Mary, 'I think genius is the power to die. In love, in poetry — how you will — but to die.' The Rector accepts and interprets the conception: 'We are in exile ... We haven't the genius to die and be reborn ... If the genius of

171

death fail us while we live, if we can't seize any of the opportunities of transcendence, then death itself will accomplish what we cannot, endowing us with the resurrection.'

For love, Morgan is not the first to use it as a theme for fiction, but not even Hardy gives it quite so prominent a position. Throughout almost the whole of each of these three novels the chief characters are obsessed by love to the extent of at least one-half of their being: the atmosphere is, nearly all the time, tense with erotic feeling. Increasingly, as we pass from the love of Nigel and Clare to that of Alison and Julie, and so to Piers and Mary, love is represented as of supreme importance to the human spirit. Nigel's love is perhaps not far from normal, except in intensity and expressiveness:

> ... for, though I was without definite anticipation of love, there was underlying all emotion a sense which I could not confess even to myself, of something shy and ardent and sacred that should be a spiritual epitome of all my secrets ... My soul lay open. I was as a deaf man in a wood of singing birds, awaiting a miracle.

Alison is a philosopher, and goes beyond feeling to belief. 'You and I,' he writes to Julie, 'were by our discovery of each other made gods with power to create, in our relationship, a perdurable essence, higher than ourselves.' Sparkenbroke is even more analytical, explaining to his wife that love was for him not affection only, however profound, nor passion only, nor a sum of these two, but an ecstasy, a dying to be reborn. To himself, thinking of Mary, he puts it thus: 'She has that quality of absolution and renewal, which is the miracle within the apparent nature of love.'

Other aspects of love are illustrated in characters who stand in vital relation to these three. Narwitz says that love is 'a form of suffering ... a form of discipline, being part of life, itself a discipline; and like all earthly gains is a designed prelude to loss'. But Narwitz had never known love as anything but suffering, and it cannot but be that he should, unlike Sparkenbroke, feel love to be 'a distraction from personal unity'. Sparkenbroke's all too pale word 'affection' in his threefold division apparently refers to the love, strongly contrasted with Sparkenbroke's, known by George Hardy. There can be little doubt that Morgan's intention, in these novels, is to present love as the ecstasy of Sparkenbroke's conception, which he finally found in Mary — or might have found if not death but Mary had kept the appointment; and it marks a quixotic courage to have allowed the rival conception so full and fair a hearing. For it might be reasonably urged that 'passionate tranquillity' is the very diagnostic of love, and as reasonably doubted whether Sparkenbroke's 'ecstasy' could give him this in enduring form. At another point Sparkenbroke distinguishes George's love as 'romanticism': writing to his wife again he says:

> One thing — I do not mean passion, for we have known passion — one thing, ecstasy, is lacking. I am seeking it always, but ... you are looking for a different element in love — what shall I call it? a supreme romanticism? You would have understood the love of the Troubadours and the Courts of Love where the bodily act was chiefly valuable neither as a pleasure nor as a means to an ecstasy beyond itself, but as a symbol of an absolute loyalty and devotion.

The letter was not sent; the passage quoted not inadequately describes George's love for Mary.

In spite of its exalted position in the Morgan narratives, love wears there, in another and more ambiguous sense than Shakespeare's, the uncertain glory of an April day, and this is particularly true of *Sparkenbroke*, where the theory of the matter is most fully displayed. Before the end, indeed, Sparkenbroke himself is sure, but he dies before he can make us sure; and up to the point when, in his last vision, he finds certainty, his assent to the inclusion of love among the three mystic revelations has been given with marked hesitation. Telling Mary that, since his childhood, he has known the radiance of reality that shines through the contemplation of death, he adds, 'there is a corresponding ecstasy to be found elsewhere ... in art, certainly; in love, I think'. He understands from the story of Tristan that 'for lovers who find it (the ecstasy of love), death has its alternative and poetry its equivalent'. But he himself has never found this ecstasy. Etty, his wife, for all her patient sympathy, could not believe he ever would, and Sparkenbroke is fretted with doubts. 'For how many years had he believed that in love was an ecstasy comparable with the ecstasies of poetry and death! How often the belief had duped him!' And yet, of course, it could come true only once, so past failures proved nothing. He knows that an incomplete love will not fulfil the conditions. 'Perhaps', he says, 'if I loved you more, if I loved you absolutely ... ' Whether or not his love for Mary ever became 'absolute' (and his double sacrifice at the end — of her as well as of himself — leaves the question unresolved), the expression is linked, at least verbally, with that other longing of his, to be 'absolved' by love (just as he felt himself, while writing, without evil, for 'to imagine was to receive absolution') — and the desire to be 'absolved' he found satisfied by Mary over and over again. Yet still, when Mary asks how, in life, the walls of the world can be made transparent (Sparkenbroke's expression for entering upon the imaginative life of death), he replies only that 'the poets are not liars'; and when she urges him, 'But in your own experience — your personal experience, apart from poetry?' he turns his head away and does not answer her. For his experience is not yet complete. And a final answer to the question whether in the Morgan philosophy love is fully co-equal with art and death as a way of entrance upon reality can come only from those who can follow Sparkenbroke and Mary imaginatively into the life they would have shared if they had gone away together that night — and if there had been no memories to come between them of others sacrificed to bring them happiness.

Or is the answer given in George Hardy (with some later confirmation from Barbet and perhaps Valerie)? George has no theories of love and of what it might miraculously do for him, but we remember how his love for Mary was described: 'that emotion towards beauty ... timeless essence ... illusion of immortality ... passionate tranquillity'. The use of the word 'illusion' might seem to rule out George's love from the Morgan scheme, but in the passage it is explicitly associated with 'desire'. And George gives some signs of having found in an utterly selfless love the miracle of peace which Sparkenbroke found in the Mound, and there is not lacking the necessary element of passion from his emotion towards Mary's beauty.

The facts which have been thus examined in *Sparkenbroke*, and which could be paralleled from the treatment of love in *Portrait in a Mirror* and *The Fountain*, seem to show a conception of love unusually high yet ever failing of its ultimate justification, and it will be interesting to continue the examination with the aim of discovering why this is so.

Morgan in the modern way, exalts the physical act of love into something that stands apart from all other forms of human experience, something of unique significance and value. As before, the conception is present throughout the three novels but is finally explicit in Piers Sparkenbroke, to whom physical union with the right woman when he finds her is to give not only 'release' but 'absolution' and a rebirth into a new life: 'the intellect denies it form, yet it's there, waiting for me, a miracle fully imagined'. The strange thing is that we are never shown this miracle in being. It is, of course, Sparkenbroke's fate to look down into the promised land but not to be allowed to enter it. But Alison and Julie enjoy a long period of regular physical intercourse. Their entering upon this relation is described in almost mystical language, and they feel they have surmounted the barrier of individuality, that all earth is made anew. Julie discovers 'tranquillity within passion itself', and Alison a new peace and continuity in his work. Yet this state endures but briefly. We find Alison despairing of his work — wondering whether it is worth while; we hear Julie insisting that there is still a barrier between them — 'the barrier is that I am I and you are you — not made to live in the same world'. And it is *before* they have become 'lovers' in Morgan's limited physical sense that Alison enunciates that exquisite appreciation of love: 'There is no surprise more magical than the surprise of being loved; it is God's finger on man's shoulder. There is no peace equivalent to the peace of loving.' For Nigel and Clare, they hack their way desperately to a physical consummation of their love at the end of the book, but it proves Dead Sea fruit. Again the final act is wrapt in mysticism and a fiery prose, but as soon as it is over there comes a sense as of something lost from the exceedingly beautiful love that has filled the book: to Nigel it comes as 'a secret questioner' who asked him 'who was she whose flesh lay there? Though, beneath the dark, she had the outward form of her I loved, she was a stranger. To consume her body would be for ever a spiritual adultery'. And before they part Nigel seems to hear Clare saying, 'Believe that I am she you loved ... You loved her in the spirit; you could not possess her in the flesh.'

In none of the three cases does physical union seem to change a fair and happy love into something fairer and happier. With Sparkenbroke we are bound to believe — if we accept the thesis of the book at all — that this result would have followed union with Mary: but what of Mary herself? Mary is drawn to Sparkenbroke with an irresistible attraction (in the circumstances could it have been otherwise?) but she has another side to her nature. 'Love, she had always believed, would be, when it came to her, a supreme sanity and reconciliation, a coming into harbour, not this blind stormy impulse that drove her to him in desperate surrender of her will.' Love as she had imagined it came to her in George Hardy, and in Italy, after she has known his love, she is aware of her duality: 'She desired the quiet of her former life [with George], which was in accordance with her nature, and that fiery percipience by which, in Sparkenbroke, her nature was lightened and magnified; above all, a harmony of these two, that she might have peace.' Once, Sparkenbroke tells her, 'the two girls met and, for an instant, became one beside the tomb of Ilaria', and were at peace. Perhaps if she had ultimately gone to Sparkenbroke the harmony would have been attained, the peace would have become lasting; but just as, with George, she cannot ever entirely forget Piers, so it may be that if she joined Sparkenbroke she would remember the utter peace and happiness of her life at the Rectory and the 'something miraculous' in the quickness of the sympathy between her and George.

In all three stories the 'miracle' of love is most nearly present before physical consummation has been achieved, and in the third one there seems very little of the miracle wanting. But in truth, although in these novels love is properly exalted to supreme poetic heights, it is never given a chance to justify itself completely, to do and be all that it is capable of under conditions approximating to ideal. Obstacles are doubtless a means to the intensification of passion, and no lover in a modern novel is deterred by the word 'illicit'; nevertheless it has to be observed that Clare, Julie and Mary are all married, and married to men for whom they entertain a very strong regard, from the sensual attraction felt by Clare towards Ned Fullaton to the strange mixture of fear and reverence that makes Julie say of her husband, 'I love him as one loves a god', and Mary's undeniably real love for George. Passion is presented as a compelling influence which there is no resisting — which, indeed, no one makes the slightest effort to resist, whatever the dangers and prohibitions; and the more antique standard is voiced only once, by that fine character, Ramsdell: 'No, Julie, I don't mean that I love you. More than the romantics suppose, love is a thing one permits or denies to oneself.' Of greater importance perhaps is the clearly recognized gulf of difference that in each novel separates the lovers. The 'portrait' of Clare received in the 'mirror' of Nigel's spirit shows her, though delightful beyond praise, still in some ways fit mate for Ned Fullaton and therefore no fit mate for Nigel Frew. Alison and Julie are to all appearances not unevenly matched, but we have seen that Julie does not feel this, and in the last pages of the book, even as they set forth for England and marriage, Alison sees 'a great division between them — a division that must increase day by day and year by year if she was to maintain her own character in its integrity and he to fight again, in the world, his battle for spiritual independence'. Between Sparkenbroke and

Mary, in spite of her intuitive insight into his poetry and her passionate and adventurous nature, there exist obvious and, one might suppose, insuperable differences. Perhaps the least of these is the difference in their ages: at the time when they meet Mary is eighteen, Sparkenbroke over thirty-three. And it is significant that this special difference is found progressively in all three novels. Alison is thirty to Julie's twenty, and there is a difference of four years in the *Portrait*. This last might not seem great enough to call for remark, but it is Nigel who is seventeen, an older but unmistakable schoolboy, while Clare's twenty-one years, especially after her marriage, give her a comparative maturity far greater than the numerical excess indicates. The ten years' difference between Alison and Julie is particularly interesting, for it is accentuated by the fact that at the age of twenty Alison was tutor to the girl of ten, so that there has been established a child-adult relation that did not quickly disappear, and for a time lent a peculiar sweetness and freshness to their love. Alison tells Julie he loves her 'with a love, hidden in me, I think, since we read of Nausicaa together'. Later he says, 'It is very strange that I did not know I loved you when you were a child. There was a quality in you then which, without my understanding it, has always stood between me and any other love but yours.' The fact that they had stood in the relation of pupil and master makes their difference of ten years almost equal to the greater one that separates Sparkenbroke and Mary. This indeed is almost terrific, for Mary is an inexperienced schoolgirl of simple family, Sparkenbroke a man of the world and of genius, of high rank and social standing, a poet and a philosopher, far-travelled and deeply lessoned in women. It gave poor Mary no chance to know whether what had come to her was love, but the point is that again we have a relation which is not one between man and woman but a relation of man to child and child to man. Deliberate intention seems to be shown by the rapid progression of the factor; it was only at times, and for a time, that Julie was a child before Alison, for through her married life with Narwitz she was a woman of experience, but all the experience was on Sparkenbroke's side, and

Mary never escaped from tutelage (not even after her marriage — and George is three years older than Sparkenbroke). The significance seems to lie here: that in these three novels, each a 'study' of a profound and intense love, and the third a presentation of love as of transcendental power, the love-relation is tinctured with an element of unreality: the loves of Nigel and Clare, of Alison and Julie, of Piers Sparkenbroke and Mary belong ultimately to faery, to the world of enchantment, of *Tristan and Iseult*; ineffably beautiful, and capable of all tragedy — except the final tragedy of all, which can only happen between man and woman.

We move a step nearer to the heart of the Morganic mystery when we turn to consider the part played by art in the trilogy. The heroes of all three novels are artists, or artist-philosophers. Nigel Frew is a painter; Lewis Alison is a historian, treating his material as an artist rather than as a scientist: he is also an artist in life and in thought; Sparkenbroke is a poet and a novelist: like Alison he is an imaginative thinker, and applies his artistic theories to life. Nigel's pictures have to be taken for granted, but we have samples, unusually satisfying, of Sparkenbroke's poetry, of his and Alison's creative thought, and of the methods of attack adopted by these two upon history and the novel. Each book shows the artist striving to maintain the integrity of his art before the invasion of life and of love. The painter, perhaps because he is so young, never gets art and love adjusted. He can keep his art only by cutting out love altogether. Only a dream-love of his own creation can be allowed to remain. 'The girl you loved has not escaped or betrayed you ... You created her in the spirit ... create her continually. Do not let her die.' Alison differs from the other two in having hardly any of that necessary ingredient in an artist's make-up — egoism; strength of character indeed is missing too. We might regard as equivocal his allowing Julie to shatter the peace of that wonderful library in the great Tower at Enkendaal, if we had not already seen him feebly releasing his hold on the heaven-sent opportunity of 'the Fort' to take part in the futile and farcical schemes of escape. In spite of these moral deficiencies he does manage to bring his art — his writing and his contemplation — under the same yoke as love; but because of these same deficiencies we remain till the end in doubt as to whether the two will combine in amity or destroy each other. All we know is that when he looks at her 'all his purposes were comprised in a single purpose — not to fail her'. In other words, he stakes all on love, and leaves his art to take care of itself. Sparkenbroke alone makes a perfect unity of art, life and love, by subordinating all else to his art, and by being the complete egoist. His egoism does not rule out a very attractive considerateness in his relations with his fellows. This is specially noticeable with his wife — a well-meaning and infinitely pathetic figure: once the supreme unkindness — that he has ceased to love her — has been set aside, his conduct towards her is unfailingly thoughtful and decent; and the same may be said of his attitude towards Bissett, the Italian doctor, young Madden, Mary and George — though in the last case again we must except the one grand injury. But more important is his absolute devotion to his art, characterized by a 'mad unsparing ruthlessness'. When Lady Sparkenbroke asks George, of her husband, 'Who is his god? What is it he wants?' George answers that he has never known Piers care for anything consistently except the perfecting of his work. He orders his life that it may subserve no other end but that of his art. 'To be engrossed by the struggle of composition ... was his happiness and his special innocence. While he wrote he felt himself to be without evil. To imagine was to receive absolution ... ' Mary broke in upon this innocence, but, unlike Alison, Sparkenbroke never allowed her, or his love for her, to deflect him for an instant from his artistic purpose. When she comes to him at the cottage, though he looks at her, his thoughts flow on round *Tristan*, and when at last he speaks to her he is unaware how time has passed. He writes more brilliantly in her love: he eagerly accepts her intuitive gleams of insight into his work; but when she leaves him to go back to her husband, apparently for ever, Sparkenbroke is able to go on to conclude *Tristan*. His final determination to take her completely into his life is motived by the knowledge that with her there will come new life, new imagination, new writing. The more astounding is his last-minute decision, subtly compounded of egoism and love, to let her go when he perceives her coming to him is not 'single-minded'.

We cannot tell what would have happened to Sparkenbroke's art if he and Mary had gone away together — what was the value of the mystical knowledge that came to him in the deathly vision while the ball at Chelmouth House was going on. But apart from this, the fear lest art should suffer loss through the coming of love is a recurrent motif. 'I feared that in my love for her I should lose my liberty', cries Nigel Frew, and, his fears materializing, he perceives his life is becoming divided — in him two dedications are opposed. So Alison, rejoicing in the miracle of the coming of leisure and freedom at Enkendaal, with thought as his natural companion, gives vent, 'against his reason, beyond his knowledge of himself', to a sudden outburst of defensive anger at the mention of Julie's name: 'Why did she want to come in?' With Narwitz, fear has hardened into a rule of belief: 'Love prevents the coming together of the soul ... all spiritual achievement is, in essence, solitary.' How unnecessary these fears, how false this belief, is surely the intention of the ultimate reconciliation effected in Sparkenbroke's vision, the truth of which we must, after all, unhesitatingly accept.

If art, or genius, has a supposititious enemy in love, it has a very real rival — an equal and opposite — in sanity; and Morgan is again fearlessly fair to the opposition. Indeed, he gives sanity such a magnificent show that there might conceivably be some doubt as to where he himself stands. Over against those characters who follow the flame of inspiration wherever it leads them — Nigel, Alison, Sparkenbroke, Julie, Mary — is set the numerically larger group of those who see a clear light and follow it steadily — Narwitz, George Hardy and the Rector, the lesser characters of Henry Fullaton, the Baron, Ramsdell, Helen and Lady Sparkenbroke, and the shadowy but intensely attractive figure of Elizabeth, Alison's first love. The two giants of the trilogy — Narwitz and Sparkenbroke — are drawn one from each side, and it would be hard to say which out-tops the other; and though Mary is divine, George holds level. He does so only by the help of his father, for he himself is a little too devoted to duty, a little un-adventurous. But he passes the critical test with honours, when Mary asks him not to leave her in Italy, but to let her go back with him to England. She cannot voice her instinctive fears, so the request appears to George utterly unreasonable, but he says to himself, This is one of the moments in which to be sensible is to be a fool; and agrees. There are a hundred marvellous things like this in George's character. And if he is still not considered quite Mary's equal, he can, as I say, call his father to his support; although indeed the sanity of that celestially bright figure, the Rector, is of an order that almost places him in the other camp, with the artists. If it were not for the intense individuality of his portrait, it might almost be considered a Christian aspect of Sparkenbroke.

We must admit that the claims of sanity are given a fair hearing, especially when we remember that Mary herself is only mad in relation to Piers. And yet, there is no sort of doubt as to the direction in which these novels face. Art is the spearhead of Morgan's faith. Sanity has a firm grip on life, but it does not know what it holds: art alone can show that. Art is 'a form of experience nearer to reality than life's own'. It is not the artist who creates, but art: art breeds new species, until life itself becomes, 'in certain aspects, a product of art'. The function of the artist is that of providing contact with this more real world behind the forms of the apparent one. Art 'gets up the curtain' on the contest between good and evil that constitutes the drama of the human spirit. Imagination, the sense of art, is the evidence of God — the King-dom of God within you. In *The Fountain* art is a little less creative: its name here is contemplation (Sparkenbroke once uses the word contemplation when he definitely means the creative act of art), but a contemplation so rapt and intense that it fulfils the function of imagination. It is not for its own sake that Alison seeks that stillness of soul, that rhythm of meditation, that singleness of spirit for which he perhaps had to accept a substitute. In its highest moods it gives him a sense of release — one of Sparkenbroke's tests for the vital movements of the soul. Like Sparkenbroke, Alison is trying to break through to that larger life, that life of the spirit, to which, he says, there is no index. The miraculous powers of art are known to Nigel Frew, and expressed with a directness suitable to youth: 'She asked me if this did not mean that I was striving to bring to a portrait the knowledge and under-standing which could belong only to God. But so I understood portraiture, I said, and indeed all art.'

It is to Sparkenbroke, naturally, that we turn for the complete expounding of Morgan's philosophy of art. And it is time to cease considering separately those three entities which we have already seen described as three aspects of the same impulse — love, art and death. They are not, in fact, treated on quite parallel lines in the novels, where love is more definitely the recreative faculty, art the approach to truth, sometimes stimulated sometimes hindered by love. Love comes in so many forms, and the false are so easily confused with the true, that even Sparkenbroke, that great lover (for a time he appears to be merely the familiar 'rake with a theory', but we know him better before the end), is dubious about the authenticity of its claims. 'For how many years had he believed that in love was an ecstasy comparable with the ecstasies of poetry and death!' He had been duped so often — taking the false for the true — that he dare not believe that Mary is to be the proof. Yet, as he feels himself, in her presence, recon-ciled after the divisions that had tormented him, he presses his eyes into the darkness of her hands, of her breast, and murmurs, 'It is the same, it is the same' — the unspeakable liberty of spirit he had known when his brother Stephen had shut him into the Mound. He had not known Mary for an hour before he was explaining to her (was ever woman — or girl of eighteen — in this humour wooed!) how three times man may understand and speak the language of the gods: 'in his love, in his contemplation and in his death'. These are his three ecstasies, his three deaths to this world that free him from the living death of the body. Is there not here, in the exalting of death, some slighting of life? Perhaps the means of access to divine truth are not quite so limited. The Rector hints at one not necessarily connected with any of the three when he says he believes that to everyone, at some time, comes the offer of the god-like nature. 'There was a moment in my life when I was capable of changing my nature, perhaps of becoming a saint.' And there are moments of freedom and happiness when the beauty of the earth becomes a transparent veil over the face of truth.

Except thus, by possible implication, there is no under-rating of life in the world of the Morgan novel. Most of his people go out zestfully to meet life. 'Life,' says Alison, 'is an inward and secret experience which those [few] who become aware of it seek to intensify, for to intensify is to protect and sustain it.' Sparkenbroke and Alison are pre-ascetics. They believe the good life is found rather in Greek joy than in Christian mortification. Both maintain that this latter was a false extension of the teaching of Jesus, which was itself allied to the Greek spirit. Once Morgan makes what seems to me a dangerous excursion beyond this position, suggesting that if only life be abundant its quality does not matter, that flesh may be abused without harm to the spirit. Perhaps Sparkenbroke has left behind his dissolute stage, and perhaps the coming of a change such as that which overcame Lord George Hell is sufficiently hinted as the intimacy with Mary proceeds, an intimacy in which, of course, asceticism plays its part.

But it is to death that Morgan's thought ultimately turns. The people of these novels are passionately interested in immortality, the greater life whose flow includes our little one. There is continual 'need to die — in love, in poetry — how you will — but to die'. Whatever art and love, in all their imperfection, may or may not accomplish, death is the culmination of their efforts, and will provide the true release, the reunion with the larger imaginative life. This phrase gives the key to Morgan's conception of life, death and immortality. Here and there he appears to make reference to pre-existence, but in truth the terms pre-existence and after-life have little meaning in a modern philosophy based on the Ouspenskian physics of time. The larger imaginative life is here, a four-dimensional world, almost within our grasp, but mortal existence, with its at least partial dependence on the bodily organs and senses, cuts us off from it. Nevertheless, in the midst of life we are in death.

It is possible for a man to penetrate some way into the regions of death, and to return to life, illuminated by gleams of a new knowledge, a new assurance. When Nigel Frew's soul is in a tumult through the loss of Clare, he climbs a hill one spring morning and lies down, face to the turf. The earth warms his isolated and frozen heart; he feels himself absorbed into the universe; he is identified with the day. He still feels utterly alone, but his solitude is the solitude of death, and 'now there was no beauty and no life save within its terrors'. He walks home, exhausted but at peace. This is the experience which, many times deepened and intensified, reappears as the miracle of rapture that came to young Piers Tenniel in the Mound. The thing happened again to Piers, a few days before his death — in that vision in which he learnt the ultimate necessity of his relation with Mary: his self is lifted from him, he ceases to feel and know in terms of temporal things; and the bars of the bird's-cage and the straight trunks of the trees in Nicodemus's forest combine to give him a sense of something more personal — 'he knew that, in his father's room, he had been gazing through the bars of the Sparkenbroke Mound, had been in his grave'. All he sees and hears thenceforward is seen and heard in the power of that exaltation.

To Narwitz also is it given to peer through the portals of death before his time has come to enter them. As he lies in bed after he has been rescued, against his will, from his terrible plight on the island, he is convinced that he had made a great part of the voyage of death before he was recalled from it, and he fears lest he may allow himself to 'slip back into life' — to forget what he has known, to accept delusion again and be no more possessed of that farther reality. The experience submits to none of the forms of thought, and cannot be described even to himself, but the spiritual impression remains, and the breath of a change is upon his eyelids. To Alison — for that most wonderful of all friendships continues even now — he tries to tell of the light that has entered into his imaginaton, showing him all the judgments of philosophy fused in wonder, and the distinguishing essence of God an infinite power of wonder. All the gains of life are a designed prelude to loss, which loss is freedom; and when this has become true for us we are baptized in wonder and are fit to die.

This is Sparkenbroke's 'will to death', which, he insists, implies no hatred of life. The world is no dungeon, but the walls go up unscalable. 'Poetry, music, mathematics, all the supreme exercises of human preception,' aim at making the walls transparent, but only in death do we pass through to what genius has seen on the further side. In another figure he tells Mary that the glitter of life's candles on the window obscures our vision of the night without.

> While they are shining in our eyes, we can see nothing beyond them. Put them out, and suddenly the night and its constellations rush in; all its distances are within reach. That is what happened in the Mound, and why I am drawn back to it ... In death, I think, the walls go down, the lights blow out; that is all, for death is not a change of state but a change of lodging; it is an incident in a continuous immortality.

I do not think Morgan anywhere suggests the Socratic and non-Christian idea that only those who have lived and died like 'philosophers' will be able to enter upon the new phase — to join the company of the gods: but as a deduction from the main conception its logic is irresistible.

The *Portrait* and *The Fountain*, alone in the Morgan series, are unhappy books, while *Sparkenbroke*, in spite of its being the only novel that is 'tragic' in the sense that it ends in the death of the 'hero', glows throughout with happy genius. The huge effort, the achieved greatness, of *The Fountain* are absent, and instead we have the rhythmic interplay of lovely characters, a Mozartian presentation of life beautifully lived. *Portrait in a Mirror* is less closely woven than the other two. There is something of a 'joint' between the two periods of Nigel's love for Clare, and there is some admission of the episodic in Miss Fullaton's portrait and the cricket match. In *The Fountain* some of the detail of the life in the Fort may be considered as of this nature, and likewise the tennis tournament, pertinent as its conclusion is to the main issue. *Sparkenbroke* is a swift unbroken stream of narrative: there is a little inconsequential detail in Book I, but nothing episodic anywhere except the Rector's expounding of the Catullus passage — an exquisite piece of work that we would not willingly lose (and the same may be said of the Fort incidents). The relevance of the classical episode is that it enables the Rector to give Mary a testimonial to Piers's character, and to provide George with a definition of his own kind of love, *sancta amicitia*.

The concluding chapters of *Sparkenbroke* have drawn some criticism upon themselves. I find only one or two small weaknesses, connected with the great technical difficulty of keeping George in ignorance of what is going on. He is made to miss seeing Sparkenbroke's car as it brings him home from abroad by the awkward device of making him stoop to pick up a stone as the car passes (Mary sees it and says nothing). The call that takes him out to old Mrs Geddes just when (with a sub-conscious sense of peril) he has determined to stay at home, seems again artificial, but coming at the moment when it does I think it convinces: at such moments of superhuman tension things do not always happen in a commonplace way; this is the justification of the incident, rather than the careful way in which it has been prepared for.

From that point everything is right. We see everything happening, and there is nothing to 'jerk you back', as Piers said, 'out of your illusion'. Morgan achieves his end by keeping us in close contact with every minutest movement of Mary's mind, and if we follow it in this way we cannot fail to be convinced that this is how things must have happened. Ever since Piers came to her, telling her they were to go away together, but imposing upon her the dreadful strain of the two days of waiting (this perhaps *is* difficult to see), her mind has been moving along two diverging lines, one part of it carrying on the life with George, the other in a conscious trance. In the wood her mind continues in this trance-like state, and in it the attempt at suicide is a natural and necessary issue of her mental processes. In a summary of the story it seems wrong: in Morgan's telling of the story (with all the queer and beautiful detail of the Theocritus!) it is absolutely right. For her mind, already bewildered and helpless, now receives a stunning shock when, hearing the approach of a car, and supposing it to be Piers coming for her, she finds it is not stopping. This shock completely unhinges her, and though those are right who say the attempt at suicide is out of Mary's character, it is not only possible but inevitable for the Mary thus transformed.

Miss Theodora Bosanquet objected to the opportune presence of the rope. 'That a well-to-do doctor's wife should have no other means of fastening a suit-case than to wind yards of thick rope round it is a predicament that needs explanation.' But if one lock of a suit-case is broken it must be fastened with either a strap or a rope. How many housewives, however well-to-do, would be able to lay their hands on a spare strap? — and Mary was debarred from asking her husband or the servants. On the other hand, odd bits of rope are always lying about in a box-room, and a piece of stout cord eight feet long (which would go twice round the case and leave the trailing end that Piers saw) fulfils all the purposes of the story.

Sparkenbroke's death itself has been attributed to 'the convenience of angina'. As well call the poisoned foil that killed Hamlet a convenience. With Sparkenbroke, as with Hamlet, 'the form of his life had been completed'. Sparkenbroke, like Hamlet, has always been possessed by the will to die: he has now lost the normal will to live, so the anticipated spasm kills him; and, like the great artist he is, he makes death come to him in the Sparkenbroke Mound.

The Voyage

A RÉSUMÉ OF the story:

In Roussignac, near Angoulême in the Charente, Barbet Hazard (thirty-two), a vine-grower and brandy distiller, is also in charge of a small prison attached to his house. Thérèse Despreux (twenty-two) is the unacknowledged daughter of Lancret, the curé. At eighteen she had run away from her aunt's place, an inn called the Cheval Pie, to be a singer and dancer, and has now returned temporarily to Roussignac, where she gives performances at the Cheval Pie. After watching one of these shows Barbet walks back, accompanied by Thérèse, to the Maison Hazard, to find the prisoners rioting under the leadership of Blachère, the only really bad one among them. Barbet quells the riot by going in to them unarmed, showing no fear, and not resisting when they attack him. His mother, who lives with him, regards this as a miracle. Barbet has been silently in love with Thérèse since she was a girl, though her life is immoral and her outlook cynical — the opposite of his. At a performance which she gives in the prison yard it becomes apparent that Barbet has an influence over her, making her for the time being good and happy. She for her part tells Barbet he is not the kind of man who ought to keep men in confinement, and suggests that he should release them. Barbet does not consider this, but tells Thérèse he loves her. She make a fanciful suggestion that they shall go away together, make a 'voyage'. This is also passed over, and Thérèse departs for Bordeaux, where she has secured a contract as a *diseuse*. Barbet presently hears that she is in Paris, and prospering.

Some months later Barbet goes to Paris on business and to look for Thérèse. By the aid of two artists, Cugnot and Madeleine, with whom he makes friends at the Ecurie Plence, he finds Thérèse in poor circumstances. He arranges for her to see Plence, a producer who runs the Ecurie, and she is given a three months' contract. Barbet and Thérèse have a day on the river, and though at first she tries to shock him by telling him about her promiscuous sex-life, by the end of the day she is happy and in a better frame of mind, admitting that she loves him.

Thérèse is living in a flat provided by Courcelet, a cultured politician whose mistress she is. She makes a striking success with a series of songs about a character she calls Barbet. She comes to give some performances in Angoulême and Barbet goes to see her. Their love grows, and she again urges Barbet to get rid of his prisoners. Departing for Royen, where she has taken a house, she thinks much about her relationship with Barbet, feeling she would like to live with him but being unwilling to give up her own way of life. She leaves the Ecurie for a more spectacular engagement at the Divertissements, and ceases to be Courcelet's mistress though they remain on excellent terms. She falls abjectly in love with a worthless person called Templéraud, and is his mistress until she finds out that he is unfaithful to her with her friend Annette. She is hit very hard but takes the blow bravely and falls back on Courcelet. She has been receiving letters regularly from Barbet, but has put them into a desk unread. Now, one night, after a talk with Courcelet, she begins to read the letters, feels strangely drawn to the writer, and learns from the last letter that he is due in Paris next day. Barbet turns up in the middle of a riotous and scandalous supper party, and by his presence and a few quiet words influences the gathering to a kindlier and more decent procedure. Barbet and Thérèse go for another steamer trip, and this time get stranded at an inn and have to spend the night together. Thérèse realizes that this is a different experience from any other she has had with men, because it is based on love.

Barbet returns to the Maison Hazard, but is restless and dissatisfied, his normal quietness of mind disturbed by the problem of the prisoners. He tries to come to terms with Blachère, but the relationship is unnatural, and when Blachère smashes some treasured belongings of the other men Barbet knows that his feelings are evil, so he opens the doors and releases the prisoners. He is now light of heart, and feels able to think about setting out on his 'voyage', to which end he sells the Maison Hazard to his brother Anton. After a time the releasing of the prisoners becomes known, and Barbet is arrested.

Thérèse tries to rouse Paris by her songs to demand Barbet's acquittal, but he is sentenced to a term of imprisonment. Nevertheless Thérèse too feels she must be free to go on a 'voyage' so she refuses a new contract. She goes to see Barbet's mother, who is in Paris and is dying. Madame Hazard has a vision of Barbet escaping from prison, and a few days later Barbet comes to Thérèse's flat, having found the door of his cell open and walked out. Thérèse continues to excite Paris by her songs about Barbet, and presently a pardon is granted on the grounds of public order. Barbet and Thérèse go on the river again, and missing the steamer they buy a sailing-boat and sail away into an unknown future, feeling that they want to be together and yet continue living independent lives. They are making their last and greatest 'voyage'.

Some comments:

If we had supposed, from Morgan's first three novels, that he was incapable of a 'hero' other than those painful introverts, Nigel Frew, Lewis Alison and Piers Sparkenbroke, we knew better when *The Voyage* appeared, and Morgan himself must have rejoiced to turn from them to the lovely and profound simplicity of Barbet. He will have felt with Frances Cornford,

> Out of the complicated house come I
> To walk beneath the sky.

Barbet Hazard is a shaggy man, wiry, short and active, with square shoulders, and is endearingly uncouth like the dog he is named after. In his brown blunt-angled face are far-looking blue eyes — 'the eyes of a northern seaman who surprisingly inhabits the body of a brown bear'. He is unaggressive and steadfast, more still than a rock, yet with the life of a bird about to fly. He has his poetry, his theory of 'voyages', a passion for wild birds and a knowledge of their ways. His vines flourish though all round him the phylloxera rages disastrously. His mother is tiny, and overflowing with caustic humour and Bonarpartism.

Thérèse has liked and trusted Barbet—ten years older—from childhood, and has delighted in the unpretentious songs he makes up. At fifteen she is taut and pliant — a birch tree, a knife in the air, and at eighteen she runs away to sing and dance for a living. Her father, the priest, is naturally unable to understand the artist's egoism that is the spring of her vitality. He complains to Barbet that when she was a child and he told her about the Crucifixion 'she was only waiting to tell you what she would have done if she had been Mary Magdalene'. Barbet, who already understands Thérèse better than she understands herself, replies that he would have liked to know what Thérèse would have done if she had been Mary Magdalene.

The prisoners, six of them (with whom, since he cannot free them, Barbet has made friends), are clearly differentiated, with Blachère the one really evil spirit: before the book is finished it would be easy to write a life-history of each of them. Indeed one quickly comes to know them so well that Barbet's quelling of the outbreak by non-resistance and a box of glow-worms seems entirely credible (the use of the glow-worms recalls the incident in Hardy where a collection of these Wordsworthian insects enabled a gambling-match to be played on a dark night on Egdon). Barbet is loved in Roussignac, but when, after four years' absence, Thérèse returns she is 'the tart from Angoulême'. We do indeed gather that prostitution is her second string, but it appears that she does it for love of the game, to satisfy the unceasing desire that is in her (she tells Barbet she needs men — 'I can't help it. It's like drink, I suppose') — and takes no money. 'Not for money, not for a contract', she tells the importunate impresario. When Victor Vincent, the cynical blackmailer, is told of this peculiarity, he sums her up, not inaccurately, as 'a romantic, an animal'. It is Victor, too, who cannot bear to see Barbet and Thérèse together, because 'life gushes from them'.

The influence of Barbet's love and personality, which is ultimately to change Thérèse's whole life, is forcibly shown at the performance she gives to his prisoners. Her act begins in bitterness and scorn, but as she goes on the spirit of Barbet, who is watching, enters her, and the nature of her singing is changed. The spontaneous bliss in him goes into her song, and she draws the prisoners to her in lightness of heart. The admirable prose of her farewell speech to her audience is unrealistic but evidently intended by Morgan, for she does it again later in the book. Barbet takes her on the river — their first 'voyage': in an exquisitely beautiful scene they listen to his swallows, he tells her he loves her — 'I believe you love all mankind', she says with irony and tenderness — and she departs for Paris, having sown in his mind the first seed of the wrongness of keeping men shut up.

A few months later Barbet too is in Paris, looking for Thérèse. He walks into the Ecurie Plence, an exclusive club and hall for artists, but is immediately accepted. And suddenly we realize that Barbet is not just a kindly countryman but a man of tremendous personality — nothing short of this would have enabled him to impress these people instantly — and of great powers of intellect and persuasion, for without effort he makes them all, including the all-powerful Plence, accept his faith in Thérèse as a *diseuse* who is not bound by any tradition but tells a story so that while she tells it it is true.

Here we meet Cugnot and Madeleine, Cugnot an original, Madeleine simply the loveliest figure in the novels. We are not given much of her, but enough to imagine the rest. I have spoken of her before but must add a touch of her quality. Barbet has told them he has no news of Thérèse, and Plence suggests 'she may be in Marseilles by now', but Barbet answers, with complete faith in his imagination, 'No, she is in Paris.'

> Madeleine's fingers closed on Cugnot's wrist. She threw back her head and laughed and sighed and said to Barbet, secretly under her breath, so that none but Cugnot heard her: 'Que Dieu te garde. Que Dieu te bénisse. Tu la verras demain.'

Next day, when Madeleine has sent for Barbet to give him some news about Thérèse, she seems to be hesitating to impart it, and Barbet wonders if she is going to tell him of Thérèse's death. 'If you have heard that Thérèse is dead, that will be wrong', he said.

Barbet buys 'some grapes, a bottle of red wine, a corkscrew, a loaf of bread, some sausage and a basket to carry them in' — and, 'something quite useless', a patch-box with lilies of the valley on the lid. He finds Thérèse and they arrange to go on the river, their second 'voyage', in the *bateau-mouche*. There is a strange pathos in their relationship, because, in spite of her swagger, she is not happy. 'Talk to me', she said. 'You tell can me the truth if you like, though even you make me angry when you disagree with me ... Tell me why you're not afraid and I am.'

It takes Madeleine to convince her that she is in love with Barbet, and when they next go 'voyaging', this time in the Gabrielle d'Estrées, though she tries (in vain) to shock him by telling him about her *amours* in the beastliest detail, she finishes the day happily, confessing she has been 'bad', and at length —

'Oh yes, I love you. Didn't you know? It's only when

I'm with you that I don't despise or defend myself. You have me as I am — even the foolish good in me — and, when you put your hand in your pocket, out comes a little box with lilies of the valley on it.'

But they agree that their lives are so different that they can never run together — 'unless one day we stopped arguing in our minds and went on and on, a real voyage'.

Barbet is back with his vines and Thérèse with her work and her lovers. When she comes to give some performances in Angoulême Barbet takes her to see his shrewd old mother, who likes her and asks if she intends to marry her son. 'Marry!' exclaims Thérèse, 'what on earth put that idea in your head?' But on the way there Barbet has taken her in his arms and kissed her, and she is at peace with his hand in hers. Again she tells him she would like to 'empty his courtyard for him', but Barbet replies gravely, 'You can't do that. Only I could do that.' He is drawing to the inevitable conclusion in this matter while Thérèse is drawing closer to him and his life. But she is drawn more ways than one. She envies Madeleine her security in Cugnot but is impatient of her absorption in Cugnot's life. Thérèse wants to live her own life, and feels her love and Barbet's can never have the ordinary natural fulfilments. Most people, she thinks, ask too much of love. Nevertheless she is imagining the possibility of changing her whole way of life. Courcelet tells her that in her thirst for popularity she is letting the rabble of her admirers play too big a part in her thoughts, and the affair with Templéraud at this time is part of the same trouble. It is as if she was making a last desperate effort to cling on to her old life, by sinking herself more deeply in it, before the new influence comes to lift her out of it. She drops to the lowest point her fine personality is capable of, and is miserable and lonely, but is saved by Barbet's letters: 'to follow with him, page by page, the movements of the year' brought her peace.

She has turned the corner, and next day Cugnot finds her transformed, enchanting, with eyes alight. She is ready for the next 'voyage', on which, by an accident that Thérèse calls a miracle, they find it necessary to sleep together. Barbet has been patient. His love, like George Hardy's, does not include desperate desire. Thérèse, too, in spite of her 'need for men', has found a sweeter relation with one man possible. She had told Courcelet, 'Everything comes naturally with Barbet. I argue with you. Not with him.' And when Courcelet had followed this up with, 'And if he wished to lie with you, Thérèse?' she had turned slowly and said with a smile, 'I argue with you. Not with him.' So it 'comes naturally', and talking about it afterwards they feel nothing is changed between them — Thérèse feels 'happy in the same way'. This is a different angle on sex from the romantic and mystical attitude that dominated the first three novels, where love expressed in sex-union was supposed to change the whole world.

Having brought Barbet and Thérèse to the point of certainty, Morgan turns to the other problem of the book. The mystical element in Barbet lies in his feeling of oneness with all people and all things: 'otherness' is foreign to his nature. While Thérèse longs for fame, Barbet feels that fame would separate him from his fellow men. Now the one thing that has flawed this unity — his troubled mind about his prisoners — is to be weeded out. Thérèse has pressed the point again (her understanding of his spiritual need is one of the miracles) and now he does what is necessary. Realizing that hatred for Blachère's violence is poisoning his mind, he goes out into the forest, lies down, and lets earth and air work upon his imagination. ('One impulse from a vernal wood', said Wordsworth.) The external process that paralleled if not occasioned the settling of Barbet's mind is described in one of Morgan's finest prose pieces:

> Great dragonflies were out hunting. A line of gold, fast narrowing in the western sky, shone through their wings as they skimmed the surface and soared abruptly against the poplars' darkness. From the opposite bank, above a reed-bed a-flutter with house-martins, over meadows sloping to the river from high ground beyond Bellis, came

the barking of a dog — a sound so remote, so small, and yet, within its tone, so clear, that it enlarged the stillness of evening. When it ceased, the distances of hearing lay open to a wide expectancy; far away a brown owl's hooting wound its long, plaintive rhythm through the dusk, to be challenged near at hand by a sudden trill of wanton splendour flung out by a robin from a neighbouring thicket. Barbet looked up and searched but could not find him. Only the brown owl continued. The poplars deepened their mass as the sky closed in upon them. Separated from the water by a bank of which the form was each instant dissolving, they and the willows appeared for a time to float in the air above the river's gleam; then to settle and stiffen to their watch. A thinning of the clouds let in a milkiness of stars which swam and vanished, and a low sheen, as of glass laid upon darkened silver, appeared on the areas of smooth water between the midstream eddies. Night flowed up and a final calm grew upon the scene.

Madame Hazard had been aware of Barbet's 'split-mind', and had felt its contrast with the 'miraculous' quelling of the early riot, when he was single-minded. When the freeing is achieved she says,

> 'You are not still troubled about anything, Barbet?'
> 'No, mother.'
> 'Ah,' she said, 'that, too, is as it should be. Now I will make some strong coffee and we will drink a glass of cognac ... After a battle and before a marriage — always a glass of cognac.'

It is amusing to observe that Barbet, now light of heart, continuing to take the money for the prisoners' upkeep, divides it equally between the Catholic and Protestant poor-boxes.

Much of the rest of the book is occupied with the arrest, imprisonment, escape and ultimate pardon of Barbet — the business is allowed to drag a little, especially over the futile machinations of the execrable Victor. When Barbet walks out of prison and comes to Thérèse, they are ready for the voyage that life has been preparing them for. They have both cut themselves loose from the old life, and are free to make a new life together if they want to. That they make it, and successfully, we need have no more doubt than we had about Gabriel and Bathsheba at the end of *Far from the Madding Crowd*.

The theme of singleness of mind has applied as much to Thérèse as to Barbet — except that what she lacked was perhaps singleness of body! Barbet was born singleminded, but had had a disruptive situation thrust upon him which he had at last — and under Thérèse's tuition — dealt with so that his mind is single as no other man's in the novels except the Judge. For Thérèse, she has known four different kinds of 'love': one of simple desire, spread over a number of men and perhaps spiritually harmless; two a 'mistress' relation with Courcelet, perhaps equally harmless; three a debased development of desire into what she horribly thinks of as 'love' — this with Templéraud; and four the growing love for Barbet, there from the beginning and coming to full flower after the story's close. The love of Barbet and Thérèse is of that abiding kind that comes of goodness, tenderness and mutual understanding, with sex as a secondary interest. It might be described as passionate and immortal friendship, and is the type of the loves of all the succeeding novels and plays except *Challenge to Venus* and *The Flashing Stream*. *The Voyage* stands not only for the blessedness of an untroubled mind, but for the supremacy of goodness and the beauty of love as against desire. I believe there are people for whom Thérèse's turning from sin is unbelievable, and who find Barbet's sinlessness dull.

CHAPTER THREE

The Judge's Story

A SUMMARY OF this novel was given in Part I (see page 57).
Comment:

The Judge's Story differs from all the other novels in being an
allegory, an allegory of the struggle between good and evil.
Evil takes the form of an immensely rich industrialist. Morgan
dislikes and fears excessive power, whether it be power over
nature, political power — dictatorship or (nearer home) the growing power of the executive, or the more insidious power of very
great wealth or collective 'finance'. Good is presented in the form
of that most harmless, and perhaps most beneficent, section of
the community, the professional class: harmless because they
cannot possibly get rich enough to exert power, beneficent (if
beneficent) because they are occupied solely with things of the
mind. The rich industrialist is George Severidge, the professional
folk are Will Gaskony, a retired judge, and Henry and Vivien
Lerrick, a young solicitor and his wife, the latter being Gaskony's
ward; with them we may put, as another representative of the
same order (though only indirectly involved), Gaskony's brother
Dick, the Oxford don.

It is only the allegorical intent that excuses Morgan's plain
portrayal of Severidge as the Devil incarnate. It is amusing to trace
the pointers. Almost Gaskony's first words to Severidge are,
'You must have been a member of the Hell Fire Club in a previous
existence', and soon he is referring to Severidge's 'infernal
memory', and thinking of his 'devilish uncomfortable effect of
drawing him out' — of tempting him, and of his look which
seemed to say, 'For me the heavens fall.' He remembers the old
monk who when he looked up from his desk always found a
little Devil looking in at the window, and on the next page,

'Severidge's face looked in at the window', though this is only Gaskony's imagination, and he has to 'put behind him' the thought of this man. Of course the Judge doesn't (yet) see Severidge as the Devil, and playfully tells Vivien 'he hasn't a cloven hoof'. Less crude are the signs given by Severidge himself of his diabolic identity. He has a habit of suddenly appearing. He will not let Vivien speak of the Kingdom of God, and is furiously angry over a sermon about the seven devils. He is sterile and dead; he is spiritually without core; he has a soundless laugh that expresses 'the embarrassments of his soul'; he would wish to take Vivien's marriage and scrawl over it. Sometimes he 'sees the whole world from within an agony of loneliness'; he confesses he cannot see any meaning in the word 'good'. He has — and this is where he is really Satanic — a great 'philanthropic' plan, backed by his money, to cultivate the liberal arts collectively, to harness 'the fatal individualism of artists' to citizenship, to guide the development of men's minds. As Vivien listens to his laying bare of his schemes, 'the vast ambition of his plan stretched before her like a desert in an insane dream'. He is also a sentimentalist and a hypocrite. His sister, who is a Christian and lives with him, knows that he is unhappy.

It is this man, polished, urbane, civilized, 'rich in intellect ... not without benevolence', who sets himself to destroy Gaskony, Vivien and Henry, specifically Gaskony. His motive? Does the Devil need a motive? Apart from mere malignancy, it is Iago's motive, the desire to tamper with a spirit finer than his own; but with Severidge there is also the sense of power. In the world of affairs he walks like a god; here is the Judge, happy in the simplicity of his life and soul — he will (as a spare-time occupation) get him too into his grasp by subtle wiles; and presently sees how Vivien can be drawn into the same net — in fact, when he begins to see that the Judge is not vulnerable in himself, Severidge conceives the idea of attacking him through his love for his ward. (Henry is already accessible, being employed by Severidge.)

The book is the story of the siege of the souls of these people, the continuous cannonade of temptation that Severidge directs at them. For Henry the bait is 'all the kingdoms of the world'; with Vivien the object is to get her to 'fall down and worship' him; with the Judge Severidge is after that end too, but turns aside to spear him on the fork of the great wager — and so loses his prize. For good weight we are given also the small but significant story of the elderly lady in Glasgow and her Cennini, which Severidge made her sell against her will. I wish Morgan had written the scene of this encounter, to match the admirable one he had already written of the preliminary interview between the lady and Henry. All we are told of this later one is that Severidge 'came out of Mrs Gorsand's presence sick at heart'.

The Judge has already succumbed (before the story opens), with almost incredible weakness, to two temptations: to accompany Severidge against his inclination on a yachting cruise, and on that cruise to tell him a part of his secret story of Julia and Vivien. Presently he is confiding to Vivien that Severidge is 'so often in my thoughts', and Vivien says she believes Severidge wants to 'change' him, to prevent him from being true to himself, and suggests that the only answer is, 'Get thee behind me, Satan'. Then come two more instances of Gaskony's strange weakness, or of Severidge's uncanny power over him. He has been telling his brother, in the empty Egg Room at Rodd's, the story that explains why he 'values that book more than anything in the world', when 'there, beyond the table, smiling and rubbing his hands, was Severidge'. 'What book?' he asks. And the Judge meekly tells him '*Marius the Epicurean*', and when Severidge banteringly and impudently goes on to ask why the book is so precious, the Judge — 'since you insist' — gives him the story in full. (Only the relation of Devil and victim can excuse the lack of verisimilitude here: a man of Gaskony's age, social standing, position and experience, would have put Severidge in his place with two words and an eyebrow.)

Severidge realizes that he now has the Judge's 'integrity' in his hands, but there is more to it than that. He would like to 'gain admittance to an individuality he envied and would be loved by'. He has within him a conflict of desire, 'to be this man's master and to be recognized and loved by him'. He tells Vivien he would value the Judge's friendship because 'it would change me: I want to be changed'—which, if it is not pure hypocrisy, affords a pathetic glimpse into the soul of the Devil.

But the Judge has by this time escaped him. There are readers who profess to find the story of the £25,000 wager too tough to swallow. The wager has been carefully led up to by the earlier jesting offer of £250 for the *Marius*, and is credibly worked up at the Club to the larger impressive figure — which is not impossibly impressive when one thinks that the previous week Severidge had probably signed a contract running into millions. To refuse to believe that the Judge would have 'sold his Marius' (and his soul) for any sum at all is not to have entered into his state of mind over the desperate situation of Vivien and Henry — the collocation of £25,000 and £23,000 is irresistible: 'I *must* sign that', he whispers, and abandons his integrity. But the Devil over-reaches himself; why, is difficult to see. To get the money back can have been no part of Severidge's original plan — he could not anticipate that Gaskony would post the book and so give him a chance to say he had never received it. Just an additional touch of malice, just an extra twist to the trap — and it opens and the victim is away, away to the safety of poverty and peace, and the Devil is left staring.

There is nothing incredible about the story of the tempting of Vivien. That she should have been attracted by Severidge at all is perhaps covered by Ledward's 'light relief' in the radio play, *The Confession*: he is accounting for Sylvia's flirting with Hugh though she loved Anstey — 'Light relief! Light relief! Women live by it. Particularly good women in love. They have to come up to breathe.' But Severidge is no common philanderer: he does not even profess to 'love' her; he wants to possess her soul, to make her fall down and worship him — and very nearly succeeds. His flattery is both subtle and strong: he calls her a wonderful woman, and compliments her on her knowledge of wine; and though she sees the flattery she is pleased that she should have evoked his 'performance'. When Henry is detained in Glasgow

Severidge invites Vivien down to his place in the country, where he lives with his sister, and she not only goes but is on the point of confiding to him Henry's financial mess when, as Severidge 'leaned forward and cocked his head for the confession', she recoils — the first of her instinctive escapes. Later she even thinks she will go to Severidge and ask him to lend them money; she gives his address to the taxi-driver—but 'with a violent movement of sudden waking' slides back the window and changes the instruction. Severidge's sister charges him with trying to seduce Vivien's soul, and warns him that 'she is pure in heart; God protects such beings from destruction'.

Now, when Henry has been rescued from the dock, Vivien begins to compare him unfavourably and unfairly with Severidge — Henry's eagerness with the older man's 'deeply founded self-assurance'. So Severidge is able to tell her — not that he loves her, that is not in his programme, but that he wants 'more than anything on earth to be loved by you'. And she lets him take her hand, but proposes they should go out—into the safety of wind and rain. She knows there is something wrong with the man, tells Henry 'we're not his kind of people', but agrees to go down with him to see 'Gasky' in his new retreat. As they search for Campion Road she stops, trying to tell him that she 'didn't want to walk across the desert, or to visit Gasky in his company, or to be thrust by his mind or his arm'. She is gaining strength to resist him, but there is still the supreme effort to be made. Severidge manages to persuade her, at the hotel, that Gaskony, whom he has seen alone, no longer wants her. He is striving with all his might for the surrender of her mind, and seems to have achieved it: her will is slipping, 'only intuition remained. She rose and left him', and does not return, but goes to have her salvation confirmed and completed by the Judge.

Vivien has already contributed to Henry's escape. His danger came when he was being drawn into the 'Severidge Foundation', the vast scheme that was to put humanity into harness to high finance. Severidge expresses his admiration for the work Henry has put into drafting a plan: 'It's as if I had been inside his mind while he worked.' But Vivien cannot respond to Henry's enthusiasm, and he too falls out and escapes.

Virtue triumphant, evil discomfited. Very unfashionable, but it does happen so, sometimes: more often in life than most people will admit, so why not in fiction, which is close to reality? Beatrice Webb wrote in her Diary in 1920: 'As I near the end of my life I become more contemptuous of cynicism, more convinced that what we know as goodness is in accordance with the nature of things.'

CHAPTER FOUR

A Breeze of Morning

A summary of the story:

David Harbrook is a schoolboy of fourteen to fifteen, working for a classical scholarship to Eton. He is by temperament, and by reason of his classical studies, mature in mind beyond his years. The owner of the neighbouring manor, Mr Letterby, who is himself a classical scholar, gets interested in David and coaches him in Latin. Presently David meets Mr Letterby's daughter Rose, a girl of eighteen to nineteen. Her mother, who had run away from her husband, and is now dead, was French and of loose morals. Rose resembles her in being 'flighty' and taking nothing seriously. David is overwhelmed by her extreme beauty; indeed his feeling that her beauty is more than mortal lasts for life and is the theme of the book. Rose accepts his worship, while declaring she is unworthy of it, and grows very fond of David. She is being courted by Dick Featherford, the good-natured but brainless heir to the local peer, Lord Comberagh, who holds a mortgage on Mr Letterby's house and estate. Living with David's family is a cousin, Howard Treladdin, an ambitious and industrious young solicitor. He is in love with, and tacitly engaged to, David's sister Ann, who is exquisitely good and kind, but he is irresistibly attracted by Rose. She for her part is carried away by his intellectual brilliance, though she recognizes that her proper mate is Dick Featherford, whom she likes but playfully despises. Ultimately Howard persuades Rose to promise to meet him at Victoria Station and go away with him to Paris, but at the last minute Rose changes her mind and sends David to Victoria to tell Howard she is not coming. She becomes engaged to Dick Featherford (now Lord Comberagh), Howard returns to Ann, and David wins his scholarship.

This summary omits:
All the detail of Rose's beauty and charm and David's adoration;
all the business of Latin between David and Mr Letterby, and of David's Latin paper in the examination;
all the charming relationship between David and his father, and between David and Ann; the episodes of the picnic, the ball, the railway porter's message, Dick Featherford and his car.

Commentary:

I do not think it can be doubted that this story is a revised version of that told in *Portrait in a Mirror*. For me also an improved version, one raised from darkness into light. The relation of Nigel with Clare began in beauty and ended in bitterness and despair; the atmosphere of the greater part of the book was one of brooding and indecision, and the conflict of art and love in the soul of the young artist almost resulted in the corruption of his art. Morgan changed all this by the simple device of lowering the age of the hero from seventeen to fourteen and making him a scholar instead of an artist. He also, less simply, transformed the heroine. Whereas Nigel's painting worked in his brain like madness, David's passion for classical scholarship kept him sane; and for Clare's sex-obsession, Rose — who is also a few years younger — is healthily and only moderately attracted by young men, charmingly by David, humorously by Dick, romantically by Howard. All the personnel are similarly made more delightful. Dick Featherford, with his tolerant 'she's a good girl, really', is a great advance on the somewhat surly Ned; David's father is a sensible and likeable person compared with the stiff parents of Nigel, and the happy relation between David and his father is one of the most enjoyable elements in the story. Henry Fullaton was good, but Squire Letterby is better and much more interesting. There is also Ann, who, with Howard, has no counterpart in the *Portrait* (except that Nigel has an unimportant sister). The main interest of the story will doubtless, for most readers, be centred in the commonplace triangle of Ann, Howard and Rose (and David himself describes his story as 'a boy's view of the love of others older than himself'), but what makes the novel unique, and a perfect expression of its title, is the coming together of Rose's beauty and essential innocence with David's youthful yet mature personality and his worship of pure beauty.*

It was sometimes difficult to believe in Nigel's profound understanding of life in terms of art; David never steps outside the

* I am aware that this view of the book is not the general one. I am told that *Portrait in a Mirror* is still the most popular of Morgan's novels, and that sophisticated people 'cannot read' *A Breeze of Morning*.

schoolboy limit. His exalted sense of the divine nature of Rose's beauty is a direct reflection of the effect of the concentrated study of Greek and Latin (which implies a considerable acquaintance with English poetry) on a mind itself attuned to spiritual overtones. But he is a schoolboy, a mixture of penetration, oddity, seriousness and humour. His chief friend is a boy whose main interest is cricket; he is excited at the thought of a night ride on an engine with his father; he is hopelessly confused by his father's explanation of the operations of Morgy Jaw and Morgy Jee, and arouses laughter in Rose by his anxiety lest she should be put bodily into the street by Dick Featherford when he takes over the mortgage. He is embarrassed before the Vicar, and generally silent in adult company because 'everything I could think of to say was too serious'. Having finished with school he — 'with a revolutionary gesture' — threw his cap out of the window, but, 'being what I am, went down into the garden, flapped the dust out of it and folded it into my pocket'.

A passage of prose, with a brilliant effect of contrast, touches off both sides of his position. As he walks to school he is wondering about Rose and her fate:

> I saw her as a fugitive, running down the avenue towards the wrought-iron gates. The avenue was a tunnel whose roof closed in upon her; her long hair streamed behind her on the night wind; the ivy stretched out its tentacles to arrest her, but she passed through them unscathed and the darkness flowed away from her, rebuked. Her face did not appear, only the sparkle of her racing eyes, bright as the spring's diadem.
>
> The door by which I entered the school led into a passage where gym shoes were kept in numbered pigeon-holes. Full of boys' shouting and the screech of nailed boots on tiles, it smelt of rubber and dust.

I have said a good deal about Rose, but must quote one more piece about her, not only because it throws a new light on her intellectual quality not elsewhere emphasized, but because it is a clever bit of writing. David and Rose are lying side by side in the punt, and she tells him that all his high opinion of her

> 'doesn't stop me wanting to turn Howard into — into — oh, you know your Shakespeare! — "the triple pillar of the world transformed — " ' '
>
> But I didn't know. *Antony and Cleopatra* was a play I hadn't read. My shame in not knowing preserves the words over forty years: 'the triple pillar of the world transformed into a strumpet's fool'.
>
> 'Oh, well,' she said, marking my silence, 'thank God for that ... '

(Rose could hardly have given David the whole quotation, and if he had known it and nodded recognition the rest of it would have been missed by those readers not remembering the passage, so David is made to have to look it up and give the complete quotation.)

In spite of Rose's matchless beauty David is the more profitable character. He is an argument for day-school education, provided the home is a good one and the education is on the arts side (I won't be answerable for science). Walking home from school he feels time and place within him like tremors of the blood and has miracles in his eyes. He has two sides to his mind, one capable of settling down to work for ninety minutes, the other of staring at irrelevant princesses and solitary towers. Having heard of Mrs Letterby's shortcomings, but knowing she was also Rose's mother, he composes an epitaph for her as he passes her grave: it is to be in Latin but is to say, 'That I was not worthless in all things, let the spring flowers and the love that planted them bear witness' — to Rose's grateful astonishment when told about it.

What gives David his place among the great figures of the Morgan world is his imaginative understanding of the mystical nature of beauty; his realization that Rose's beauty has a more than human significance; that it is the visible semblance of godhead, a mortal sign of immortal reality. But there is also something admirable and endearing in his warm human love for his sister

Ann. 'My love of her, of her purity of heart, came down upon me like a calm.' The placing of the two girls — both perfect in their different ways — in juxtaposition is a masterstroke of the novelist. David has spoken of Rose's beauty being a mask for divinity; now, seeming to change the metaphor, he speaks of mask and face as what romantics and realists respectively see, and saying, 'neither mask nor face is a lie', he adds, 'my sister is the only person I have known whose mask and face have seemed to me identical. She is what she appears to be; she is undivided'. Coleridge spoke of Shakespeare's dramatic tact in never letting Ariel and Miranda appear together, and though Morgan does not quite follow suit he takes care that Rose and Ann shall not come into direct opposition. Twice, at a tennis-tea and at the picnic, they are both present, but only a word or two is recorded as having passed between them. On the occasion when there would have been a contrast that might have been shattering to both — when Ann wants to go to the Manor and 'have it out' with Rose over Howard — David firmly steps in to forbid the fatal encounter (it is part of his 'magic' that he is always 'there' when his presence can be helpful).

But the theme of the book is David's mystical love for Rose, and as an undertone, and accompaniment, there runs the theme of his classical studies, his secondary preoccupation with his Eton Scholarship. This culminates in the scene of the examination itself, with its miraculously achieved set of Latin elegiacs. The scene makes an exquisitely framed episode, and some of the most memorable parts of the book are of this episodic nature: the picnic, the porter's message and the way David follows it up; even the story of Howard and Rose seems to me a rather large detail in the impressionist picture that is David's vision, the vision of Rose printed on his imagination at his first sight of her leaning over from the gallery, and never fading or changing afterwards. When all is long past, and Rose married and dead, David explains to Ann that he had seen a quality in Rose which no one else saw, and which has formed part of his inner life ever since. 'Some people', he told Ann, 'are lucky; they go into the house. And some remember what they saw through the window. They are not unfortunate — if they do remember, clearly and faithfully.'

Like *The Voyage, A Breeze of Morning* is a study in innocence. Can there really be any who think life is more truly seen in Mr Graham Greene's frightful Boys than through the clear eyes of David Harbrook?

CHAPTER FIVE

The Burning Glass

THE PLOT:

Christopher Terriford, in charge of a weather-station, has invented a machine, and 'hit upon' a setting of it, by which the sun's rays can be focused as through a lens, then reflected and brought to bear on any region of the earth with such power that everything in that region is burnt up. The formula for the setting is a secret know only to Christopher and his wife, Mary. England is being threatened by a foreign totalitarian power, and the question arises of whether he should allow this new weapon to be used in defence of the country. The Prime Minister, who happens to be staying in the neighbourhood, is asked to come for consultation. Christopher explains and demonstrates the power of his discovery, but says (*a*) that he will not let the secret of the setting out of his own possession, (*b*) that he will be willing to set the machine if it becomes necessary in war, (*c*) that he will not allow the new power to be used in peace, industrially, at all. Before the argument with the Prime Minister is settled, Christopher is kidnapped and carried off by the enemy foreign power. Mary and Christopher's assistant set the machine, and two areas of the foreign power's territory are destroyed as a warning, and Christopher is returned to his home. He still refuses to allow the Burning-glass, as the device is called, to be used other than in dire necessity of war, his reason being that he believes that the possession of excessive power over nature is corrupting to the human mind.

Comments:

Like the novel, the play can get along perfectly well without a moral or a meaning. But it is not obstructed by having such a moral or meaning, provided the requisite art goes into the writing. A play may well have an intellectual content to its artistic shape, and *The Burning Glass* is a play of this sort. We are following an argument as well as a story.

The moral or political theme is clearer and more absorbing

than that of either of the two earlier plays. It was easy to sit through *The Flashing Stream* without realizing that in Commander Ferrers' refusal to yield to pressure from his superiors we were to see a virtue called singleness of mind, and I doubt whether 'Heron', who embodied the philosophic idea of *The River Line*, was sufficiently distinguishable among his fellows to drive the idea home. This is not to decry the two plays in any way: they are, in their narrative and dramatic action, altogether admirable, but I think *The Burning Glass* is a better play in these respects also. The dramatic crisis of *The Flashing Stream* comes when the efforts to perfect what we now call a ground-to-air missile seem to have failed, and there is danger of the research unit being closed down. The situation is given conflict and suspense but it is not in itself enthralling. *The River Line* has two crises: the first, the sudden killing of one member of a group of friends by the others, is exciting but shocking; the other, the discovery by the murdered man's sister of what had happened to him, and the consequent setting free of a love-relation, is a little difficult to come at by reason of its psychological complexity.

But there is no mistaking the desperate importance of the problem confronting the actors in *The Burning Glass* — whether a new and tremendous source of power which the hero of the play has discovered is to be used for destructive purposes, for promoting man's material welfare, or for both these ends. During the First Act we are gradually acquainted with the nature of this force, in the Second we understand the inventor's scruples about its use, in the Third we see the inventor's wife holding by his scruples even while her husband is in the hands of the foreign power against whom his invention might be a protection: the climax comes when, having been released by reason of a display of the efficacy of the new power, he dramatically returns — to continue the argument. His belief, passionately held, is that the growing power of man over nature is something devilish, and that man is not godlike enough to control it — hence he will do nothing to speed the degeneration.

But this is only the intellectual ghost of the play, the flesh and blood of which are constituted by a group of characters brilliantly and lovingly conceived, and presented in a series of dramatic situations. Christopher Terriford is a scientist with a conscience, a figure we can believe in, though it seems to have no counterpart in life. His conscience would not have operated so effectively, would have surrendered, like the others, to scientific tradition, had it not been vitalized by Mary, his wife. It is she who (in the prologue, which does not get on to the stage) suggests that he should 'let his new discovery go'. 'You mean, forget it? Never communicate it to anyone? No man of science has ever killed power. Can I do that?' 'If it is devilish', she said, 'you have to.' That is a very simple statement, morally unimpeachable and logically indisputable. Yet it takes a woman to make it, and her husband, who loves her, to accept it.

Mary Terriford is more than a clear thinker with an instinctive sense of right and wrong: she is entirely human and infinitely delightful. Morgan's feeling for her is shown in his stage-direction:

> She is beautiful and gentle, simple and direct; so full of happiness and peace that nothing shakes her. The roots of her life are her love of God, which saves her from panic in the upheavals of the world; her love of her husband, which gives her vitality and balance; and her sense of proportion, which prevents her from condemning human frailty, even Tony Lack's.

We see her in the first act dealing with Tony's evidently genuine (though doubtless 'romantic') love for her with exactly the right degree of firmness and kindness, as we see her in the last act accepting his suicide with perfect compassion. She only once puts a foot wrong — and this is Morgan's fault not hers. Later in Act I Tony is pressing his attentions, and she asks, 'What, in reason, do you want?' He replies in a flash, 'To go to bed with you.' How Mary *would* have dealt with that request I am content to leave to her, but what she certainly would not have said is what Morgan makes her say — 'Why do you want to go to bed with me?' And when Tony includes among his 'reasons' that she 'would be charming naked', Mary is made to say, 'There are other women as good — naked. Why do you want me?'

No comment, except that this is a blotch of black paint that Morgan dropped on to his canvas, and it has to be cleaned off before we have Mary unspoilt.

Tony himself is not altogether unfit to make love to Mary. Christopher explains his vagaries — his solid early home had 'crumbled when he was a fighter-pilot', he had married 'a good girl' and she had been killed, he 'no longer has a personal life that he in the least minds losing'. Had time permitted, Mary might have healed his soul and made something of him, as Candida was going to do for Eugene — but he has got himself involved with the real bad man of the piece, Gerry Hardlip, brilliant cosmopolitan adventurer, complete cynic and immoralist, a star economist in the pay of an unscrupulous power, 'an intellectual cosh-boy by nature'. Tony is a child in his hands, and lets slip the information that results in Christopher's being kidnapped by Hardlip's gang and in Tony's having to 'go out of harbour under his own steam'.

Lady Terriford, Christopher's mother, hovers in the background, as mothers do in plays, but to better effect than most. She and Maria Guerina are the only entirely admirable mothers in the novels and plays — it is interesting that they appear in the last novel and the last play.

So we come to the Prime Minister, Montagu Winthrop, whom — distinct personality as he was — we saw as an interpretation of our own great war-leader. He is so big and vital that he would have stolen the thunder from anyone but Christopher and Mary and Lady Terriford. As it is he plays his part in the great chess-game — knight, bishop and rook in one, but leaving the glory of king and queen undimmed. He takes — as politicians and even statesmen are bound to do (which is why the knowledge of dangerous scientific discoveries should be kept from them) — he takes the purely practical and patriotic view of the Burning-glass: here is a weapon to give Britain 'absolute mastery', a force with which to drive more and bigger machines. But he has a mind capable of seeing Christopher's point of view when he wants to keep the formula, the setting, in his own hands, whereas Henry Strait, the commonplace politician, is furious at the very suggestion. There is good 'theatre' in Christopher's explanation of the watertight method he has devised for ensuring secrecy — 'half the setting deeply planted in my wife's memory, the other half in a sealed envelope in the hands of a friend, a village doctor ... In emergency, if I am absent, Mary will telephone him and give him a code word. He will post the letter. The two halves of the setting will come together'.

The Prime Minister makes a fine speech to show his understanding of Christopher's dilemma, but concludes by saying it is only a question of 'sacrificing an ideal', of 'acknowledging that our conscience is not infallible'. But Christopher and Mary still believe that the consequences of sacrificing their ideal will go far beyond themselves, and feel that their conscience is a better guide than the conditioned reflexes of a War Minister. So, while Christopher is absent in enemy hands, Mary continues to insist that to corrupt life is a greater evil than war. She would, under the Prime Minister's gentle but inexorable pressure, have yielded half-way, but Christopher comes dramatically back and resumes command. And he still, for the reasons given, refuses the use of the Burning-glass as an instrument of industrial power in time of peace. He declares moreover that he believes the 'originating minds', and the people too, would be with him, that 'the whole era of Power for Power's sake is near its end'. This was a long-term hope: the years that have passed since the words were written have seen little to justify the hope.

The battle fades and the Prime Minister goes up to bed, with a whimsical comment on the unfinished chess-game as he passes it set out (again) on the table: the impression of the spiritual strife remains with us, because it has been carried on by such a memorable group of people, and brought to life by a close-knit dramatic action. It is noteworthy that in this last of his plays, almost the last of his writings, Morgan should have presented some of his deepest and sanest thought through four of the very finest of his characters, with one of them a 'perfect woman, nobly planned', and with the one example in the whole of his novels and plays of a perfect marriage.

About that chess-game. Is it symbolic of the battle of wits that had gone on, with Gerry Hardlip knocking over the pieces and 'ruining their game' in the middle of the play but helpless against Mary's genius that restored order and renewed the game before the end? Or is it, as I prefer to see it, a symbol of the peaceful, absorbing life of that beautiful home, that 'citadel' against which all the confusions of the outer world battered in vain, and which continued, an eternal verity, when the politicians and the plotters had had their say and gone?

INDEX

INDEX

INDEX

INDEX

DATE DUE

GAYLORD			PRINTED IN U.S.A